# ADVANCED
# TECHNOLOGY
# IN
# CRITICAL CARE
# NURSING

Edited by
## John M. Clochesy, MS, RN, CS
Veterans Administration Medical Center
West Los Angeles, California

Aspen Series in Critical Care Nursing
Kathleen Dracup, Series Editor

AN ASPEN PUBLICATION®
Aspen Publishers, Inc.

1989

Rockville, Maryland
Royal Tunbridge Wells

Library of Congress Cataloging-in-Publication Data

Advanced technology in critical care nursing.

"An Aspen publication."
1. Intensive care nursing--Technological innovations.
I. Clochesy, John M. [DNLM: 1. Critical Care--nurses' instruction.
2.Nursing--instrumentation.     WY 154 A244]
RT120.I5A38     1989     610.73′61     88-8114
ISBN: 0-8342-0023-6

The authors have made every effort to ensure the accuracy of the information herein,
particularly with regard to drug selection and dose. However, appropriate information
sources should be consulted, especially for new or unfamiliar procedures. It is the
responsibility of every practitioner to evaluate the appropriateness of a particular
opinion in the context of actual clinical situations and with due consideration to new
developments. Authors, editors, and the publisher cannot be held responsible for any
typographical or other errors found in this book.

Editorial Services: Marsha Davies

Library of Congress Catalog Card Number: 88-8114
ISBN: 0-8342-0023-6

*Printed in the United States of America*

1  2  3  4  5

To my family, Ralph, Lill,
Colleen, Pat, and Myk.

# Table of Contents

**Contributors** . . . . . . . . . . . . . . . . . . . . . . . . . . . . . . . . ix

**Preface** . . . . . . . . . . . . . . . . . . . . . . . . . . . . . . . . . . . . xi

**Chapter 1— Historical Development of Technology
and Critical Care Nursing. . . . . . . . . . 1**
*John M. Clochesy*

The Past . . . . . . . . . . . . . . . . . . . . . . . . . . . . . 3
Today . . . . . . . . . . . . . . . . . . . . . . . . . . . . . . 9
The Future . . . . . . . . . . . . . . . . . . . . . . . . . . . 9

**Chapter 2— Clinical Computer Systems . . . . . . . . . . 13**
*John M. Clochesy*

The Problem . . . . . . . . . . . . . . . . . . . . . . . . . . 15
Current Approaches . . . . . . . . . . . . . . . . . . . . . 16
Future Directions . . . . . . . . . . . . . . . . . . . . . . . 17

**Chapter 3— Bedside Monitoring. . . . . . . . . . . . . . . . 21**
*John M. Clochesy*

Current Practice . . . . . . . . . . . . . . . . . . . . . . . . 23
Continuous Blood Gas and Electrolyte
  Monitoring . . . . . . . . . . . . . . . . . . . . . . . . . . 23
Continuous Glucose Monitoring . . . . . . . . . . . 25
Intragastric pH Monitoring . . . . . . . . . . . . . . . 25

**Chapter 4— Advances in Mechanical Ventilation . . . 29**
*Verna Medina*

Types of Ventilators . . . . . . . . . . . . . . . . . . . . 31
Ventilator Modes. . . . . . . . . . . . . . . . . . . . . . . 32
Pressure Support Ventilation . . . . . . . . . . . . . 35
Inverse Ratio Ventilation . . . . . . . . . . . . . . . . 38
New Generation Ventilators . . . . . . . . . . . . . . 42

**Chapter 5— Pulse Oximetry . . . . . . . . . . . . . . . . . . 51**
*Susan Joy Nelson*

Principles . . . . . . . . . . . . . . . . . . . . . . . . . . . 53
Clinical Application. . . . . . . . . . . . . . . . . . . . . 56
Clinical Operation . . . . . . . . . . . . . . . . . . . . . 57
Display Screen . . . . . . . . . . . . . . . . . . . . . . . . 58
Sensor. . . . . . . . . . . . . . . . . . . . . . . . . . . . . . 58
Potential Problems . . . . . . . . . . . . . . . . . . . . 59
Patient Care Considerations . . . . . . . . . . . . . . 61
Accuracy. . . . . . . . . . . . . . . . . . . . . . . . . . . . 61
Case Studies . . . . . . . . . . . . . . . . . . . . . . . . . 64
Summary . . . . . . . . . . . . . . . . . . . . . . . . . . . 66

**Chapter 6— Noninvasive Cardiac Output**
**Determination . . . . . . . . . . . . . . . . . . 69**
*Mary Woo*

Doppler Technology . . . . . . . . . . . . . . . . . . . . 72
Transthoracic Electrical Bioimpedance . . . . . 75
Summary . . . . . . . . . . . . . . . . . . . . . . . . . . . 79

**Chapter 7— Continuous ST-Segment Analysis . . . . . 83**
*John M. Clochesy*

Significance. . . . . . . . . . . . . . . . . . . . . . . . . . 85
Application . . . . . . . . . . . . . . . . . . . . . . . . . . 86

**Chapter 8— External Pacemakers** . . . . . . . . . . . . . **89**
　　　　　　 *John M. Clochesy*

　　　History of External Pacemakers . . . . . . . . . . .  91
　　　Pacemaker Characteristics . . . . . . . . . . . . . .  91
　　　Effectiveness of External Pacing. . . . . . . . . . .  94
　　　Myocardial Injury . . . . . . . . . . . . . . . . . . .  94
　　　Implementing External Pacing . . . . . . . . . . . .  94


**Chapter 9— Automatic Implantable Cardioverter-**
　　　　　　　 **Defibrillator** . . . . . . . . . . . . . . . . . . . **99**
　　　　　　 *Carol M. Mravinac*

　　　The AICD System . . . . . . . . . . . . . . . . . . . . 101
　　　Different AICD Models. . . . . . . . . . . . . . . . . 102
　　　Indications . . . . . . . . . . . . . . . . . . . . . . . 104
　　　Contraindications . . . . . . . . . . . . . . . . . . . 106
　　　Methods of Implantation. . . . . . . . . . . . . . . . 106
　　　Preoperative Preparation . . . . . . . . . . . . . . . 107
　　　Postoperative Care . . . . . . . . . . . . . . . . . . . 108


**Chapter 10—Cardiac Assist Devices** . . . . . . . . . . . . **119**
　　　　　　　 *Richard A. Henker and Danni Brown*

　　　Pulmonary Artery Balloon Pumping. . . . . . . . 121
　　　Ventricular Assist Devices . . . . . . . . . . . . . . 126
　　　The Total Artificial Heart . . . . . . . . . . . . . . 132
　　　Summary . . . . . . . . . . . . . . . . . . . . . . . . . 137


**Chapter 11—Continuous Ultrafiltration Therapy. . . . 141**
　　　　　　 *Alice Whittaker*

　　　Technical Design and Setup . . . . . . . . . . . . . 143
　　　Determinants of Ultrafiltration . . . . . . . . . . . 146
　　　Anticoagulation of the Ultrafiltration Circuit . 150
　　　Continuous Ultrafiltration Modalities . . . . . . . 151
　　　Summary . . . . . . . . . . . . . . . . . . . . . . . . . 154

**Chapter 12—Closed-Loop Medication Delivery Systems**.........................**157**
John M. Clochesy

**Chapter 13—Economic Considerations of New Technologies**....................**163**
John M. Clochesy

Perform Economic Assessment ........... 165
Determination of Real Cost............... 166

**Chapter 14—Technology, Ethics, and Critical Care . . 169**
Ginger Schafer Wlody

Current Health Care Environment ......... 171
Societal Changes....................... 173
Identification of Ethical Conflicts .......... 176
Factors Affecting Ethical Issues and Ethical Decision Making ..................... 183
Role of the Nurse in Addressing Ethical Issues.............................. 187
Framework for Addressing Ethical Issues ... 188
The Future ........................... 194
Summary ............................. 194

**Index.**....................................**197**

# Contributors

DANNI BROWN, RN, MS, CCRN
Staff Development Clinician
  El Dorado Hospital & Medical Center
  Tucson, Arizona

JOHN M. CLOCHESY, MS, RN, CS
Clinical Nurse Specialist
  Veterans Administration Medical Center
  West Los Angeles, California
Adjunct Professor
  California State University
  Long Beach, California

RICHARD A. HENKER, RN, MS, CCRN
Critical Care Educator
  University Medical Center
  Tucson, Arizona

VERNA MEDINA, MN, RN
Clinical Nurse
  UCLA Medical Center
  Los Angeles, California

CAROL M. MRAVINAC, MN, RN
Clinical Nurse
  Cedars-Sinai Medical Center
  Los Angeles, California

SUSAN JOY NELSON, BS, RN, CCRN
Clinical Nurse
  UCLA Medical Center
  Los Angeles, California

ALICE WHITTAKER, MS, RN, CCRN
Director of Clinical Nursing
  University Medical Center
  Tucson, Arizona
Adjunct Assistant Professor of Nursing
  University of Arizona
  Tucson, Arizona

GINGER SCHAFER WLODY, RN, MS, CCRN
Nursing Quality Assurance Director
    Veterans Administration Medical Center
    West Los Angeles, California
Assistant Clinical Professor
    University of California
    Los Angeles, California

MARY WOO, MN, RN
Doctoral Student
    University of California
    Los Angeles, California

# Preface

Over the past 2 decades, technology used in monitoring and treating critically ill patients has become increasingly complex. Major advances have been made in cardiovascular, respiratory, and renal therapies. Other technologies permit closer monitoring and supportive care. Microprocessors (computer chips) are responsible for many of the advances. Formal training for nurses does not focus on physics, bioinstrumentation, mechanics, electronics, or fluidics. If newer biomedical devices are to be applied effectively, those caring for the critically ill must understand the principles on which these devices are based.

The book is divided into three parts. The growth of technology within the history of critical care is traced in Chapter 1. In Chapters 2 through 12 emerging technology and its application to patient care are described. The economic and ethical issues that accompany the increasing use of resource-intensive technology in the care of the critically ill are explored in Chapters 13 and 14. Critical care instructors, clinical specialists, and experienced critical care nurses will find this book useful as a reference for self-review and as a resource for staff development and inservice programs.

# CHAPTER 1

# Historical Development of Technology and Critical Care Nursing

*John M. Clochesy*

# 1

## THE PAST

Current critical care nursing practice and biomedical technology used in patient care have been influenced by many social and historical events. For example:

- Antibiotics were first developed during World War II.
- The poliomyelitis epidemic of the 1940s and 1950s led to the research that resulted in the development of newer forms of mechanical ventilation.
- Mobile army surgical hospitals (MASH units) and helicopter transport of the sick and injured first were used during the Korean Conflict.
- Discoveries during the manned space program led to development of complex physiological monitoring and telemetry equipment.
- The Vietnam War and the Highway Safety Act of 1966, with its extension in 1971, necessitated developments in trauma care.

Specific historical developments are identified in the chronology of technology and critical care presented in Table 1-1.

The staffing in early intensive care units (ICU) varied greatly. In 1953, one hospital provided 9.6 direct hours of nursing care per patient day (HPPD). This direct care was provided by a combination of registered nurses and licensed practical nurses. In 1963, care was provided by all registered nurses, by registered nurses and licensed practical nurses, or by registered nurses, licensed practical nurses, and nursing assistants. Hours of nursing care per

**Table 1-1** Chronology of the Development of Technology and Critical Care

| Date | Event/Discovery |
|---|---|
| 1820 | • First successful blood transfusion performed by Blundell at Guy's Hospital in a woman suffering from postpartum hemorrhage |
| Late 1800s | • Stethoscope, thermometer, roentgenograms developed |
| 1891 | • First spinal tap reported |
| 1902 | • Surgeons attending a meeting in Cleveland question what the measurement of blood pressure has to do with the practice of surgery |
| 1913 | • Patient-triggered, pressure-cycled ventilator constructed by Janeway |
| 1920s–1930s | • Wagensteen suction first used |
| 1920 | • Intravenous lipid solution introduced |
| 1923 | • Neurosurgical intensive care unit established at Johns Hopkins Hospital |
| | • First peritoneal dialysis performed by Ganter |
| 1924 | • Oxygen tent made of rubberized silk |
| 1925 | • First physician in United Kingdom diagnoses myocardial infarction |
| 1928 | • Iron lung manufactured for Dr. Drinker of Harvard by the J. H. Emerson Co. for use at Boston Children's Hospital |
| 1929 | • Cardiac catheterization first used |
| 1937 | • Intravenous amino acid solution introduced |
| 1942 | • Curare introduced |
| 1940s–1950s | • Manual ventilation via tracheostomy replaced chest cuirass |
| | • First human dialysis performed |
| 1947 | • Positive end-expiratory pressure (PEEP) used |
| | • Cardiac massage and open-chest defibrillation first successfully applied |
| 1948 | • Intermittent positive-pressure ventilators (IPPV) developed by Bird and Bennett |
| 1951 | • Heideman and Harken establish ICU at Peter Bent Brigham Hospital |
| | • Guillaume and Janny demonstrate rationale for continuous intracranial pressure monitoring |
| 1952 | • External cardiac pacing developed |
| 1953 | • Multidisciplinary medical-surgical ICU delivering 9.6 hours of care per patient day by registered nurses and licensed practical nurses established at North Carolina Memorial Hospital |
| | • Gibbon and associates construct cardiopulmonary bypass machine |
| 1954 | • First successful organ transplant (kidney) performed in a human, from one twin to his brother |
| 1956 | • First closed-chest alternating-current defibrillation used |
| 1958 | • Mouth-to-mouth artificial respiration advocated |
| | • Transvenous pacing developed |
| | • Multidisciplinary ICU opened at University Hospital in Baltimore |
| 1960s | • Permanent arteriovenous shunt developed |
| | • Arteriovenous fistulas developed |

**Table 1-1** *(Continued)*

| Date | Event/Discovery |
| --- | --- |
| | • Artificial grafts for vascular access used |
| 1960 | • Prosthetic heart valves developed |
| | • Closed-chest cardiac massage developed at Johns Hopkins Hospital |
| 1962 | • First four coronary care units (CCUs) were established: Sydney, Kansas City, Toronto, Philadelphia |
| 1963 | • The Joint Committee on the Accreditation of Hospitals solidly supported ICUs; director Dr. Kenneth B. Babcock predicts "it's only a matter of time" before an intensive care unit standard appears in the accreditation manual. |
| | • Admission and discharge criteria were biggest problems according to a survey of 450 hospitals |
| 1965–1971 | • Articles appear about the stress of ICU nursing |
| 1967 | • First human heart transplant performed by Barnard in South Africa |
| | • Pulmonary oxygen toxicity acknowledged |
| 1968 | • American Association of Neurosurgical Nurses (now American Association of Neuroscience Nurses) established |
| | • Intra-aortic balloon pump developed by Kantrowitz and associates |
| 1969 | • American Association of Cardiovascular Nurses (now American Association of Critical-Care Nurses) established |
| 1970s | • Computed tomography (CT) developed |
| 1970 | • Flow-directed balloon-tipped pulmonary artery catheter developed in Los Angeles at Cedars-Sinai Medical Center by Swan and Ganz |
| | • Society of Critical Care Medicine founded |
| 1971 | • Recommendation that monitoring of acutely ill cardiac patient include: electrocardiographic (ECG) monitor, pulsimeter, and toe temperature was published |
| 1972 | • *Heart & Lung* first published |
| 1973 | • *Critical Care Medicine* first published |
| | • AACN membership neared 10,000 |
| | • Emergency drugs available in prefilled syringes (Bristojet) |
| | • GE Patient Data System developed with recall of previous 1, 4, 8, and 24 hours of physiological data |
| | • Hydraulic ICU beds introduced |
| | • PhysioControl introduced Lifepak-3 with a non-fade screen, charge button on paddles, and quick look as exclusive features |
| | • AVCO IABP Model #7 with three-chamber balloon introduced |
| | • Experimental transvenous defibrillator used |
| 1974 | • AACN's first National Teaching Institute held in New Orleans |
| | • Low pressure cuff tracheostomy tubes developed by Shiley |
| | • Esophageal obturator airway introduced |
| | • Right ventricular infarct recognized as distinct entity |
| 1975 | • Aero-Flo suction catheter to reduce suction-related trauma introduced by Argyle |
| | • Nitroprusside introduced |
| | • Pressure bag used for constant infusion |

*Continues*

**Table 1-1** *(Continued)*

| Date | Event/Discovery |
| --- | --- |
| | • Model 9510 Cardiac Output Computer for use with Swan-Ganz flow-directed balloon-tipped pulmonary artery catheters developed by Edwards Laboratories |
| | • Transfusion filter developed to protect from microemboli |
| | • IVAC 530 infusion pump and IVAC 230 infusion controller introduced |
| | • Computerized arrhythmia monitoring system introduced by Gould |
| | • Manual resuscitation bag with oxygen reservoir advocated by Laerdal |
| | • PhysioControl Lifepak-4 and Datascope M/D2 defibrillators introduced |
| | • Modified chest lead I ($MCL_1$) recommended |
| | • Medical Personnel Pool recruited nationally |
| | • Urimeter urinary drainage bags used |
| 1976 | • Disposable laryngoscopes introduced |
| | • Wood's first pulmonary artery pressure/patient positioning study published |
| | • IMED volumetric controller developed |
| | • Independent nurse educators began providing continuing education as a business |
| | • Disposable transducer domes introduced |
| | • Disposable Yankauer suction catheter developed |
| | • Noninvasive nuclear medicine cardiac imaging introduced |
| | • Hope II manual resuscitation bag with oxygen reservoir introduced by Ohio Medical |
| | • Medtronic temporary demand pacemaker Model 5880A and atrial pulse generator (50-800 ppm) Model 5320 developed |
| | • Incentive spirometers first used |
| 1977 | • Bear 1 volume ventilator developed |
| | • Gould/Statham cardiac output computer introduced |
| | • Dinamap noninvasive blood pressure monitor introduced |
| | • Dopamine first used |
| | • Cath-'n-sleeve suction catheter used |
| | • Argyle Salem Sump nasogastric tube used |
| | • Datascope single-chamber balloon IABP introduced |
| | • Hewlett-Packard ear oximeter developed |
| | • Disposable defibrillator pads first used |
| | • AVCO Model #10 IABP introduced |
| | • Edwards Model 9520 cardiac output computer developed |
| | • Metal carts designed and sold for resuscitation supplies |
| | • Powaser-Guthrie's first article on endotracheal suctioning published |
| 1978 | • Medtronic temporary pacemaker Model #5375 developed |
| | • Hillrom "power column" introduced |
| | • Datascope M/D3 defibrillator developed |

**Table 1-1** *(Continued)*

| Date | Event/Discovery |
|---|---|
| 1979 | • Siemens arrhythmia monitoring system introduced |
| | • Cephalothin (Keflin) introduced |
| | • Flurazepam (Dalmane) introduced |
| | • IMED 960 volumetric controller developed |
| | • Hibiclens (chlorhexidine) replaced hexachlorophene as hand-washing agent for hospital personnel |
| | • Dobutamine introduced |
| | • Molter's study on needs of family members published |
| | • IVAC 630 volumetric infusion pump developed |
| | • Bretylium introduced |
| | • PhysioControl Lifepak-6 defibrillator developed |
| | • Central station monitors in color with ability for the user to put messages in each patient's area introduced by Midwest Analog & Digital |
| | • Arrow complete introducer kit first used |
| 1980s | • Magnetic resonance imaging (MRI) developed |
| | • Cyclosporine (immunosuppressant) introduced |
| | • Nafcillin, carbenicillin, cefamandole, cefoxitin, mezlocillin, piperacillin, amiodarone, mexiletine, and tocainide introduced |
| 1981 | • Hemochron 400 (ACT) developed |
| | • PhysioControl Lifepak-7 developed |
| | • Interest renewed in autotransfusion |
| 1982 | • First permanent total artificial heart (Jarvik-7-100) implanted by DeVries at University of Utah |
| 1984 | • Baboon heart transplanted in infant with hypoplastic left heart syndrome |

patient day ranged from 10.3 to 31.5 in units with all registered nurse staffing. The 15.5 hours of nursing care per patient day were reported in units with a combination of registered nurse and licensed practical nurse staffing, whereas units with registered nurses, licensed practical nurses, and nursing assistants reported 11.3 to 17.1 hours of nursing care. Modern ICUs deliver from 12 to 26 hours of direct nursing care per patient day.

In 1963, a survey was done of the 450 hospitals known to have established ICUs. Each hospital was asked what equipment its ICU had. Results of this survey are summarized in Table 1-2. That same year, health care professionals at Cedars of Lebanon, a teaching hospital in Los Angeles, published the process that they followed in establishing its ICU. The equipment present in its ICU is listed in Table 1-3.

**Table 1-2** Equipment in Intensive Care Units—1963: A Survey of 450 Hospitals Known To Have ICUs

| Equipment | Percent of Hospitals |
|---|---|
| Oxygen therapy equipment | 100 |
| Oxygen and suction outlets | 92 |
| Laryngoscope | 92 |
| Respirators | 86 |
| Cardiac pacemaker | 85 |
| External-internal defibrillator | 78 |
| Bronchoscope | 76 |
| Electrocardiograph | 73 |
| Hypothermia blanket | 72 |
| Cardiac monitor | 70 |
| High humidity oxygen tents | 70 |
| Portable operating room light | 51 |

During the 1960s nurses began to specialize and recognized the need to develop professional associations for support and education in specialized nursing practice. The American Association of Cardiovascular Nurses, now the American Association of Critical-Care Nurses, was formed in 1969. Critical care nurses have kept aware of rapidly developing technology through their journal, *Heart & Lung*, and through lectures and exhibits at annual teaching institutes.

**Table 1-3** Equipment in the Intensive Care Unit, Cedars of Lebanon Hospital, Los Angeles—1963

Cardiac pacemaker
Internal-external defibrillator
Pump oxygenator
Respirators
Intermittent positive-pressure valve
Facilities for dialysis and "assisted circulation"
Oximeter
Cardiac monitor
Thermister unit
Gastric hypothermia unit
Anesthesia machine
Electrocardiograph

The past 3 decades may be summarized as periods of development of resuscitative measures: 1950–1960 as the decade of respiratory resuscitation, 1960–1970 as the decade of cardiac resuscitation, and 1970–1980 as the decade of brain resuscitation.

## TODAY

In the 1980s and 1990s we continue to see the development and refinement of complex cardiopulmonary support technology. Other therapeutic technology is being refined. Physiological monitoring is becoming less invasive, and the clinical laboratory is being moved to the patient's bedside. In the remainder of this book we will explore the technological advances and ethical questions facing us today.

## THE FUTURE

Technology of the future should provide less risk to patients while maximizing the productivity of nurses, physicians, respiratory therapists, and other members of the critical care team. American Zettler, a manufacturer of hospital nurse call systems, described the nurse of 1990 in an advertisement as one who wears:

- a nursing cap beret given on graduation from nursing school in Silicon Valley
- a name tag with an identity chip listing specialty education and training, while automatically recording actual nursing hours
- a two-way radio transceiver on the uniform collar to answer or cancel patient calls by voice activation
- a state-of-the-art wristwatch that measures time in milliseconds, including an automatic distance-measuring device since premium bonuses will be paid for excess distance traveled
- non-slip shoes with built-in battery-operated vibrator soles.

Patients will be wearing a noninvasive probe taped to their skin that will record temperature, pulse, and respiratory rate for the entire shift.

Priorities of critical care biotechnology for the next decade must include integration of systems, data input and access by voice activation and recognition, feedback-control systems, and expert systems to assist in diagnostic and treatment decisions.

**BIBLIOGRAPHY**

Beck CS, Pritchard WH, Feil HS: Ventricular fibrillation of long duration abolished by electric shock. *JAMA* 1947;135:985–986.

Beck CS, Weckesser EC, Barry FM: Fatal heart attack and successful defibrillation: New concepts of the coronary artery disease. *JAMA* 1956;161:434–436.

Bower AG, Bennet VR, Dillon JB, et al: Investigation on the care and treatment of poliomyelitis patients. *Ann West Med Surg* 1950;4:561–582, 686–716.

Bruce DA: *The Pathophysiology of Increased Intracranial Pressure: Current Concepts.* Kalamazoo, Upjohn, 1978.

Cadmus RR: Special care for the critical case. *Hospitals* 1954;28(9):65.

Delano A, Carrel B, Shubin H, Weil MH: Monitoring the acutely ill cardiac patient. *Cardiovasc Nurs* 1971;7(1):61–64.

Fortune G: Positive pressure therapy. *Am J Nurs* 1947;47:108.

Furman S, Robinson G: Use of an intracardiac pacemaker in the correction of total heart block. *Surg Forum* 1958;9:245–248.

Goldman J, Bassin P, Sandler S: We combined intensive and recovery units. *Mod Hosp* 1963;100(1):79–83.

Green HL, Hieb GE, Schatz IJ: Electronic equipment in critical care areas: Status of devices currently in use. *Circulation* 1971;43:A101–A122.

Harken DE, Taylor WJ, LeFemine AA, et al: Valve replacement with a caged ball valve. *Am J Cardiol* 1962;9:292.

Hilberman M: The evolution of intensive care units. *Crit Care Med* 1975;3:159–165.

How to prepare for intensive patient care. *Mod Hosp* 1963;100(1):70–78.

How to provide the best intensive patient care. *Mod Hosp* 1963;100(1):67.

Intensive care units produce transfer and staffing problems, survey shows. *Mod Hosp* 1963;100(1):68–69.

Jude JR, Elam JO: *Fundamentals of Cardiopulmonary Resuscitation.* Philadelphia, FA Davis Co, 1965.

Jude JR, Kouwenhoven WB, Knickerbocker GG: External cardiac resuscitation. *Monogr Surg Sci* 1964;1:59.

Kampschulte S, Safer P: Development of a multidisciplinary pediatric intensive care unit. *Crit Care Med* 1973;1:308–315.

Kantrowitz A, Tjønneland S, Krakauer JS, Phillips SJ, Freed PS, Butner AN: Mechanical intraaortic cardiac assistance in cardiogenic shock. *Arch Surg* 1968;97:1000–1004.

Kinney JM: The intensive-care unit. *Hosp Topics* 1967;45(4):89–99.

Kouwenhoven WB, Jude JR, Knickerbocker GG: Closed chest massage. *JAMA* 1960;173:1064–1067.

Masson S: Surveys show need for intensive care. *Mod Hosp* 1963;100(1):94–95.

McCulloch J, Townsend A, Williams DO: History and development of coronary care units, in McCulloch (ed): *Focus on Coronary Care*. London, William Heinemann Medical Books, 1985.

Milstein BB: *Cardiac Arrest and Resuscitation*. London, Lloyd-Luke Medical Books, 1963.

Nash G, Blennerhassett JB, Pontoppidan H: Pulmonary lesions associated with oxygen therapy and artificial ventilation. *N Engl J Med* 1967;276:368–374.

Norcross MD: The Drinker respirator. *Am J Nurs* 1939;39:1200.

Phillips GD: Life support systems in intensive care: A review of history, ethics, cost, benefit and rational use. *Anaesth Intens Care* 1977;5:251–257.

Rockwood CA, Mann CM, Farrington JD, Hampton OP, Motley RE: History of emergency medical services in the United States. *J Trauma* 1976;16:299–308.

Safar PJ: Mouth-to-mouth emergency artificial respiration. *JAMA* 1958;166:1459.

Starr A, Edwards ML: Mitral replacement: Clinical experience with a ball-valve prosthesis. *Ann Surg* 1961;254:726.

Swan HJC, Ganz W: Hemodynamic monitoring: A personal and historical perspective. *Can Med Assoc J* 1979;121:868–871.

Thevenet A, Hodges PC, Lillehei CW: The use of myocardial electrode inserted percutaneously for control of complete atrioventricular block by artificial pacemaker. *Dis Chest* 1958;34:621–631.

Travis KW, Carson S, Uhl RR, Bendixen HH: Report on the first year's activities of a multidisciplinary respiratory intensive care unit. *Crit Care Med* 1973;1:235–238.

Weil MH: The Society of Critical Care Medicine, its history and its destiny. *Crit Care Med* 1973;1:1–4.

Wheeler DV: How we trained intensive care nurses. *Mod Hosp* 1963;100(1):90–91.

Zoll PM, Linethal AJ, Gibson W, Paul MH, Norman CR: Termination of ventricular fibrillation in man by externally applied electric countershock. *N Engl J Med* 1956;254:727–732.

# Clinical Computer Systems

*John M. Clochesy*

# 2

## THE PROBLEM

Over the past 2 decades, computers and computerized monitoring equipment have invaded critical care units.[1] Each of these devices promised to be "new and improved" at whatever its function. Computerized systems have been developed to

- detect dysrhythmias
- measure urine output and flow
- report lab results
- calculate medication infusion rates
- monitor vital signs
- enter medical orders
- admit, discharge, and transfer patients
- prepare unit time schedules
- plot cardiac output of artificial ventricles
- organize and locate patient records and x-ray films
- retrieve drug and poison information
- monitor inventory levels
- generate care plans
- calculate nutritional requirements and order patient trays and supplements
- document care.

In most hospitals, each of these devices or "systems" is independent of the rest. As the use of these devices increases, nurses perform increasing amounts of work to achieve the same outcome. At a time when there is a serious mismatch between the supply and demand for critical care nurses, these systems should decrease the demand on nurses' time.

Computerized systems will increase productivity of caregivers in the ICU only when they are integrated and the caregivers discontinue duplicate manual systems. For example, nurses do not graph vital signs manually, nurses do not transcribe physician's orders, and so on. Several hospitals and hospital systems are trying to develop integrated systems.

## CURRENT APPROACHES

Since 1980, the University Hospital, State University of New York at Stony Brook, has been developing the University Hospital Information System (UHIS). Today it has both clinical and administrative components. It is built around a single dual-processor mainframe computer with several large disk and tape drive units and a network of 300 terminals and 100 printers.[2] The minicomputers that support the Physiological Monitoring/Patient Data Management System for 92 critical care beds have been networked to the UHIS system.

Shabot and associates in the surgical ICUs at Cedars-Sinai Medical Center in Los Angeles have developed their system around bedside Hewlett-Packard Monitor-Terminals and the HP Patient Data Management System.[3] In addition to the bedside monitor-terminal with key pad, standard video display terminals (VDTs) are located between every two patient rooms. The challenge with such arrangements is to send data from the laboratory, pharmacy, and admission-discharge-transfer (ADT) systems back to the patient's bedside monitor.

Humana Hospital Suburban in Louisville, Kentucky, is piloting Health Data Sciences' Ulticare system with a VDT at every patient bedside. Although this system when fully implemented will integrate most hospital information system functions, physiological monitoring remains separate. It is impractical to keep a VDT and a computerized monitor-terminal at each patient's bedside.

Several vendors are developing portable terminals to be carried from bed to bed by the nurse. Examples include the NCR 1601 Portable Nursing Unit Terminal (PNUT), the Marquette Electronics'

Electronic Patient Information Chart (EPIC), and Motorola's EMTEK system 2000.

The PNUT is a notebook-sized battery-operated device that is carried from bedside to bedside. After the nurse visits patients and makes the appropriate notations, the PNUT is placed into its holder/charger. While in the holder/charger, the stored data are downloaded into the hospital's patient information system. Although innovative and potentially useful in a less technology intensive environment, the PNUT does not automatically collect data from other electronic devices.

The EMTEK and EPIC systems automatically record vital signs from the bedside monitor or telemetry. The nurse may validate or correct the information when time permits. These systems provide gateway processors to translate data from one information system to another. Through these gateways, laboratory and pharmacy systems can send important information directly to the bedside.[4]

## FUTURE DIRECTIONS

The goals of critical care information management are to

- automate the steps in creating the patient record
- collect data *once* from the person responsible for it
- collect data automatically from the source whenever possible, including physiological data from the bedside monitor and laboratory data from the laboratory computer system.[5]

Systems of the future must be based on Standards of Critical Care Practice established by the American Association of Critical-Care Nurses (AACN) and the Society of Critical Care Medicine (SCCM). They should facilitate expert systems using chosen taxonomies [e.g., North American Nursing Diagnosis Association (NANDA)]. All systems under development should remain "open systems" based on communication between numerous microcomputers and microcomputer-based monitors and devices.

Future systems must provide for remote access to the system. Physicians need to check on their patients from their homes or offices. Satellite clinics need access to centralized records, especially the results of diagnostic tests. Digitized images replacing standard x-ray films could be viewed in the same way. "Filmless" radiology departments are being developed by joint ventures between large radiology equipment vendors and university teaching hospitals. It is estimated that up to 20,000 standard x-ray images will be able to be stored on a single 12-inch optical disk. Lost films will no longer be problematic, nor will there be problems of several people trying to view the same image simultaneously.

On discharge, a given patient's record could be converted into a permanent unalterable form. Although some hospitals will prefer to continue to keep "paper" charts, storage space and risk of damage or destruction could be dramatically reduced by writing the patient's chart on an individual optical diskette that could be kept on file indefinitely in a small storage area. This record could include all electrocardiograms, electroencephalograms, and x-ray images. After a given period of time, inactive patients' data could be purged from the on-line database. Should an inactive patient be readmitted, his or her record could be reloaded to the on-line database from the optical diskette.

Although the future is not yet here, it is important to insist that any equipment purchased be directly compatible with existing monitoring/communication systems or that the equipment contain a standard computer output port.

---

**REFERENCES**

1. Weil MH, Shubin H, Rand WM: Experience with a digital computer for study and improved management of the critically ill. *JAMA* 1966;198:1011–1016.

2. Vegoda PR, Dyro JF: Implementation of an advanced clinical and administrative hospital information system. *Int J Clin Monit Comput* 1986;3:259–268.

3. Replogle KJ: A computer at every bedside: Issues and obstacles. *Crit Care Nurs* 1986;6(1):14–21.

4. Marquette Electronics: *EPIC: Electronic Patient Information Chart,* 1987.

5. Brimm JE: Computers in critical care. *Crit Care Nurs Q* 1987;9(4):53–63.

**RECOMMENDED READING**

Clochesy JM, Henker RA: Selecting computer applications in critical care. *Dimens Crit Care Nurs* 1986;5:171–177.

Gardner RM, Hawley WL: Standardizing communications and networks in the ICU, in Association for Advancement of Medical Instrumentation (AAMI): *AAMI Proceedings of Monitoring Conference,* 1984.

# Bedside Monitoring

*John M. Clochesy*

# 3

## CURRENT PRACTICE

Traditionally, blood samples and other specimens are obtained periodically and sent to the clinical laboratory. In the treatment of the critically ill patient there is a need for rapid or continuous determination of certain blood chemistries. Rapid determination requires that whole blood samples be used. Because of the large quantity of blood taken for diagnostic tests, some patients require replacement transfusions. These transfusions have the risk of transfusion-borne viral diseases such as non-A, non-B hepatitis.

To decrease the time from sample collection to treatment decision based on the results, nurses in many critical care units periodically draw and run samples for determination of blood glucose, hematocrit, activated clotting time, and, in some cases, arterial blood gases in their own "stat lab." These technologies may yield results that correlate highly with the clinical laboratory when used by an experienced operator ($r = 0.92$ to $0.95$).[1] Several technologies are being developed that will allow continuous monitoring of many of these chemistries, which will provide trends and reduce the amount of time nurses spend preparing and running samples. Personnel in clinical laboratories will no doubt continue to perform chemical profiles and more specialized tests.

## CONTINUOUS BLOOD GAS AND ELECTROLYTE MONITORING

Continuous monitoring of various blood chemistries is being made possible by developments in microelectronics and fiber-optics. Ion-sensitive field-effect transistors (ISFETs) make it possi-

23

ble to measure electrolytes whereas fiberoptic systems make it possible to measure oxygen saturation using photoluminescence-based technology. Major research efforts on the development of microsensors include the development of dissolved gas and pressure sensors to be used within blood vessels.[2]

## Development of ISFETs

The ISFET is an insulated gate field-effect transistor. When the sensor is placed in a solution, an electrical potential is generated at the solution–gate insulator interface. The gate circuit is completed by a reference electrode. The measured ISFET current drain measures the electrolyte activity at the solution–ISFET interface. An ion-selective membrane is placed over the ISFET gate so that it measures the activity of only the desired ion.[3] Intravascular pH sensors are currently being tested.[4] Fifteen patients following coronary artery bypass grafting had pH catheters placed into the femoral artery. The catheters were flushed continuously with a heparinized saline solution. After a 60-minute stabilization period, blood was drawn through the lumen of the catheter. The pH monitor was then calibrated to the results. Once calibrated, the results correlated well with intermittent blood gas measurements. The catheters were removed at 12 hours, and there were no signs of clot formation or protein deposition over the sensor.[5]

Studies of two intra-arterial oxygen sensors have been published.[6,7] One electrode is made of silver/silver chloride, and the other is made of platinum. Both electrode–monitor systems correlated very highly ($r = 0.98$) with $Pao_2$ values from concurrent blood gas analysis.

Shortly pH, oxygen, and potassium ion sensors will be common, and their results will be displayed on the bedside and central station monitors. Other ion sensors, such as ionized calcium, will also become available. Development of the sensors has taken significant research effort to deal with

- need for frequent calibration
- potential for thrombogenesis
- sterilization of the electrode contributes to sensor instability
- mass production techniques.[8]

## Optical Fluorescence

Initially, fiberoptic systems were used for continuous mixed venous oxygen saturation ($Svo_2$) monitoring. Several intra-arterial oxygen and blood gas systems are being tested. Two reports on American Bentley's "optode" sensor show correlations between it and arterial blood gas analysis to be 0.956 to 0.970 in the range from 0 to 800 mm Hg.[9,10] The correlation under 200 mm Hg, the area of clinical usefulness, however, is much lower. Further development will be required before this sensor can be used clinically.

Another fiberoptic system measures pH, $Pco_2$, and $Po_2$. Correlations with concurrent blood gas analysis were very good ($r = 0.97$, 0.95, and 0.92, respectively). There were no clinical differences in the values obtained by the intra-arterial system and standard blood gas analysis.[11]

## CONTINUOUS GLUCOSE MONITORING

Determination of the blood glucose level is the only study other than blood gas analysis and measurement of electrolytes that is critical on a continuous basis. Work continues on the development of an implantable coated-wire glucose sensor.[12] Such a sensor could help in the management of critically ill diabetics in ketoacidosis and may lead eventually to the implantation of an artificial beta cell that delivers insulin on a continuing basis based on serum glucose levels.

## INTRAGASTRIC pH MONITORING

Nasogastric sump tubes and feeding tubes have been introduced that have antimony pH electrodes at the tip (Figure 3-1). The pH probe can assist in placement of the tube. There is a normal path of pH as the tube passes, much as one watches for specific waveforms during insertion of a pulmonary artery catheter. In the nose, pharynx, and esophagus the pH ranges from 5.8 to 6.0. As the tube enters the stomach the pH drops to 1.8 to 2.0 unless the patient has recently received antacids or $H_2$ blockers, in which case the pH will be 3.5 to 4.5. If a stomach tube accidentally moves into the duodenum, or if a feeding tube is being placed, the pH rises to 6.8 to 7.1. If

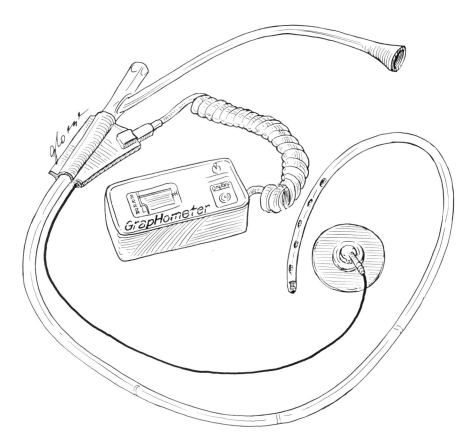

**Figure 3-1** GrapHprobe ST nasogastric tube with built-in pH probe and attached pH meter.

the tube finds its way into the lungs during insertion, the pH reaches 7.3. Several studies awaiting publication will recommend using pH measurement to check tube placement, avoiding routine chest x-ray films.

Use of these probes will allow for tube placement and proper titration of antacids and $H_2$ blockers to prevent stress ulceration or bacterial overgrowth caused by excess alkalinity. Other benefits include the ability to monitor gastric pH continuously without the need to obtain gastric aspirates. This saves caregivers' time and reduces exposure to body fluids.

**REFERENCES**

1. Ting C, Nanji AA: Evaluation of the quality of bedside monitoring of the blood glucose level in a teaching hospital. *Can Med Assoc J* 1988;138:23–26.

2. Esashi M, Matsuo T: Solid-state micro sensors. *Med Prog Technol* 1987;12(3–4):145–157.

3. Eberhart RC, Thomasson TH, Munro MS, Kumar A, Szabo G: Indwelling chemical sensors based on semiconductor technology. *Crit Care Med* 1982;10:841–847.

4. Bergveld P: The development and application of FET-based biosensors. *Biosensors* 1986;2(1):15–33.

5. Van Der Starre PJA, Weerd JEH, Schepel SJ, Kootstra GJ: Use of an arterial pH catheter immediately after coronary bypass grafting. *Crit Care Med* 1986;14:812–814.

6. Green GE, Hassell KT, Mahutte CK: Comparison of arterial blood gas with continuous intra-arterial and transcutaneous $Po_2$ sensors in adult critically ill patients. *Crit Care Med* 1987;15:491–494.

7. Katayama M, Murray GC, Uchida T, Shindo M, Tanaka T, Miyasaka K: Intra-arterial continuous $Po_2$ monitoring by an ultrafine microelectrode. *Crit Care Med* 1987;15:357.

8. Sibbald A: Chemical biosensors and on-line patient monitoring. *Med Instrum* 1985;19:164–167.

9. Barker SJ, Tremper KK, Heitzmann HA: Continuous fiberoptic arterial oxygen tension in dogs. *Crit Care Med* 1987;15:403.

10. Barker SJ, Tremper KK, Heitzmann HA: A clinical study of fiberoptic arterial oxygen tension. *Crit Care Med* 1987;15:403.

11. Shapiro BA, Cane RD, Chomka CM, Gehrich JL, Tusa JK: Evaluation of a new intra-arterial blood gas system in dogs. *Crit Care Med* 1987;15:361.

12. El Degheidy MM, Wilkins ES, Soudi O: Optimization of an implantable coated-wire glucose sensor. *J Biomed Eng* 1986;8:121–129.

**RECOMMENDED READING**

Barker SJ, Tremper KK: Intra-arterial oxygen tension monitoring. *Int Anesth Clin* 1987;25(3):199–208.

# Advances in Mechanical Ventilation

*Verna Medina*

# 4

Mechanical ventilators have been used for several years to support patients with respiratory failure. The earliest models used negative pressure. The "iron lung" created a vacuum around the chest wall, increasing its diameter. The resulting negative intrathoracic pressure caused air to enter the lungs. These ventilators were often cumbersome and have been replaced by positive-pressure ventilators.

There have been significant developments in positive-pressure ventilators. These advances came about because of an increased understanding of the physiology of breathing and powerful microprocessor technology. Commonly used modes of mechanical ventilation are reviewed here, and newer ventilatory support modes and ventilator technology are introduced.

## TYPES OF VENTILATORS

Types of ventilators currently in use include pressure-cycled, volume-cycled, and time-cycled ventilators. Pressure-cycled ventilators deliver a flow of gas until a preset pressure is reached. The disadvantage of this type of ventilator is the variable delivery of tidal volume depending on changes in airway pressure and lung compliance. Pressure-cycled ventilators may be used in patients who have no preexisting pulmonary disease and who will not resist the support of mechanical ventilation.

Volume-cycled ventilators are the most commonly used ventilators in the critical care setting. These ventilators deliver a preset tidal volume. Tidal volume is calculated to yield 10 to 15 ml/kg of body weight. The advantage of volume-cycled ventilators is that a consistent tidal volume will be delivered despite a change in the patient's lung compliance. There is, however, a safety mechanism known as a pressure limit, which stops air flow when an excessively high peak inspiratory pressure is reached.

Time-cycled ventilators are a refinement of pressure-cycled ventilators. These machines deliver a flow of gas for a specified amount of time. However, the pressure to deliver this gas does not exceed a preset pressure limit. Time-cycled ventilators are used most often in pediatric patients.

High-frequency ventilation (HFV) is another method of providing ventilatory support. This method uses high ventilatory rates and low tidal volumes to maintain alveolar ventilation. Rates are generally greater than four times the normal rate (> 60 breaths per minute), and tidal volumes are often less than the volume of anatomic deadspace. There are three basic modes of delivering HFV:

1. High-frequency positive-pressure ventilation for rates up to 100 breaths per minute
2. High-frequency jet ventilation (HFJV) for rates up to 600 breaths per minute
3. High-frequency oscillation for rates up to 4,000 breaths per minute

Theoretically, HFV increases diffusion of oxygen and carbon dioxide by increasing molecular kinetic energy. A purported benefit of HFV is the reduction of barotrauma and the decreased cardiac output that accompany positive-pressure ventilation. Its use has been reported in a variety of clinical situations including bronchopleural fistula.

**VENTILATOR MODES**

Ventilator controls allow for a variety of functions and modes. In the control mode of ventilation, the tidal volume is delivered by the ventilator at the set rate regardless of the patient's inspiratory effort. This mode is rarely used. In the assist mode, a preset volume is delivered when triggered by the patient's negative inspiratory effort. If the patient stops initiating breaths, no ventilation will occur. Because of the potential for this problem, a modification of assist mode, assist/control (A/C) mode, was developed.

In the A/C mode, if the patient's respiratory rate falls below a preset level of support, the ventilator automatically enters the control mode. All breaths, initiated by the patient or ventilator, are of a preset tidal volume. The advantage of this mode is that it guarantees a preset minute ventilation and also allows the patient to trigger the ventilator for additional breaths.

In the intermittent mandatory ventilation (IMV) mode, the patient is provided with a preset number of breaths at a given tidal volume by the ventilator (control mode). However, the patient is allowed to breathe spontaneously through the ventilator circuit between the mandatory breaths. These spontaneous breaths are not assisted breaths, and the tidal volume will vary depending on the patient's ability to generate negative pressure. IMV or positive-pressure ventilator breaths are completely independent of the patient's breathing pattern. IMV does not take into account whether the patient's spontaneous breath is in inspiration or expiration. Subsequently, synchronized intermittent mandatory ventilation (SIMV) was developed to deliver the mandatory breaths in synchrony with the patient's inspiratory negative trigger. SIMV is also known as intermittent demand ventilation (IDV).

The SIMV mode of ventilation allows the patient to assume some work of breathing and prevents weakening of the respiratory muscles. SIMV facilitates weaning from mechanical ventilation. By reducing the number of mandatory breaths, the patient must gradually take over the work of breathing. Since the increased work of breathing may fatigue the respiratory muscles, T-tube weaning or the newer pressure support mode may be needed to wean some patients.

Positive end-expiratory pressure (PEEP) is another function offered by most ventilators. PEEP is continued pressure maintained in the airway and alveoli at the end of each breath. PEEP improves arterial oxygenation and gas diffusion capacity by reexpanding and preventing alveolar collapse. PEEP can be used concurrently with any of the previously mentioned modes of ventilation. Continuous positive airway pressure (CPAP) is the application of PEEP in spontaneously breathing patients. CPAP is most often applied using an endotracheal tube, face mask, or nasal mask. Improved oxygenation, similar to PEEP, occurs from this therapy. For this reason, CPAP is frequently used during the weaning process. Airway pressure in various ventilator modes is diagrammed in Figure 4-1.

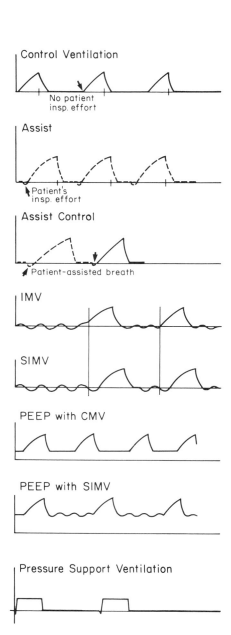

**Figure 4-1** Airway pressures in various ventilator modes.

Pressure support ventilation (PSV) and inverse ratio ventilation (IRV) are the newest ventilatory modes. These modalities hold much promise and will be presented here in greater detail.

## PRESSURE SUPPORT VENTILATION

Pressure support ventilation is a new mode of assisted ventilation that supports spontaneous breathing in patients who are receiving mechanical ventilation. In this ventilatory mode, the patient's spontaneous inspiratory effort is augmented with a selected amount of positive airway pressure. Like other ventilator assist modes, the patient must be able to generate negative intrathoracic pressure (inspiratory effort) to open a demand valve for delivery of pressure support. As long as the patient maintains an inspiratory effort, gas will be supplied at the preset constant pressure. PSV is delivered as a plateau of positive airway pressure throughout the patient's inspiratory effort, differentiating it from intermittent positive-pressure breathing (IPPB). This plateau effect eases flow of gas into the lungs and increases tidal volume (Figure 4–2). In effect, the ventilator performs some of the work of breathing in a spontaneously breathing mode. PSV is terminated when a certain minimum inspiratory flow is achieved.

Unlike A/C or SIMV modes, PSV allows the patient to regulate his or her own ventilatory rate, tidal volume, and inspiratory flow rate and time because only the airway pressure is selected. Because of this, the tidal volume will vary depending on the patient's ventilatory effort. The level of PSV may be adjusted to maintain a certain tidal volume.

### Effects of PSV

Little information exists about the cardiovascular and respiratory effects of PSV. It is hypothesized that PSV may have an effect on ventilatory mechanoreceptors and muscle function.[1] Mechanoreceptors in the lungs and thoracic cage sense changes in stretch. As these changes are relayed to the ventilatory control center in the central nervous system, ventilatory rate, tidal volume, and inspiratory flow adjust to provide optimal gas exchange for the least amount of work. Any change in ventilatory mechanics can

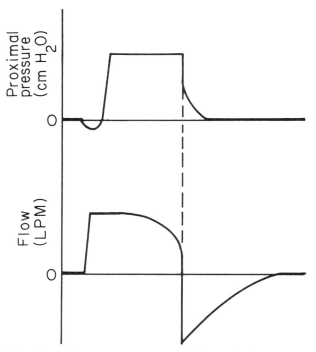

**Figure 4-2** Proximal airway pressure and flow during pressure support ventilation.

alter this input-response system to cause the patient to experience dyspnea and/or asynchrony with the ventilator ("bucking"). Since pressure support allows the patient to control the ventilatory pattern, this mode may stimulate the mechanoreceptors in a way similar to normal spontaneous breathing, thus reducing patient discomfort and dyspnea.

The effect of PSV on respiratory muscle function remains unclear. It is postulated that PSV alters the work of breathing.[1] The diaphragm, the primary respiratory muscle, works against airway resistance and lung compliance to maintain the necessary minute ventilation. In the presence of various disease conditions, airway resistance and/or lung compliance can be affected, resulting in an increased workload on the diaphragm. With excessive amounts of work, the diaphragm can fatigue. When respiratory failure occurs, mechanical ventilation is usually begun to allow the overworked muscles to rest and recover. The passive respiratory muscles can atrophy, however. Therefore, an appropriate amount of muscle work is necessary to prevent atrophy and to provide muscle conditioning for later weaning.

The nature of A/C, SIMV, and T-tube trials may not result in optimal muscle conditioning. In these modes, the respiratory muscles work only when the patient spontaneously breathes without assistance from the ventilator. The amount of work is usually greater since the patient must work against airway resistance (artificial airway, ventilator circuit, and demand valves) and the residual effects of the disease condition (e.g., decreased lung compliance). Supporting spontaneous breaths with a constant pressure can lower airway resistance and reduce the patient's respiratory muscle work. By adjusting the amount of pressure support, the work of breathing can be controlled to avoid fatigue.

Other effects of PSV include decreased activity of the diaphragm, as reflected by lower transdiaphragmatic pressure (pressure generated by the diaphragm during spontaneous inspiration.)[2] The reduction in diaphragmatic activity lowers oxygen consumption and ventilatory rate while increasing tidal volume. A study of PSV in 14 patients following cardiac surgery revealed an increase in minute ventilation but no adverse effects on cardiovascular and respiratory variables.[3] Another study looked at the effects of pressure support on hemodynamic and respiratory variables. It found no consistent change with pressure support levels up to 30 cm $H_2O$.[4] Increasing pressure support levels results in decreased patient work of breathing with increased tidal volumes, decreased ventilatory rates, constant minute ventilation, and increased patient comfort.[1]

## Indications for PSV

PSV is considered for patients who have difficulty weaning from mechanical ventilation using conventional methods. Patients who generate small tidal volumes are apt to develop fatigue and thus can benefit from the PSV effects of improved tidal volume and decreased work of breathing. Patients may easily fatigue if they are not able to generate the inspiratory effort needed to open demand valves or overcome airway resistance. Airway or ventilatory circuit resistance can increase the work of breathing and result in patient fatigue, exhaustion, and early termination of weaning. Inability to wean can cause anxiety and frustration in both patients and caregivers. In many instances, PSV can be adjusted to overcome airway resistance, deliver the desired tidal volume, and allow gradual increases in respiratory muscle work by the patient. When adequate ventilation results at a pressure support level as low as 5 to 8 cm $H_2O$, extubation should be considered.

PSV is helpful in patients who are highly anxious and/or asynchronous with the ventilator. Since PSV enables the patient to determine ventilatory rate, tidal volume, and inspiratory time and flow, sedation requirements decrease. Patients who have limited respiratory or cardiac reserves can also benefit from PSV. In these patients, increased work of breathing can be harmful because it results in an oxygen demand that cannot be met. PSV lowers oxygen demand during respiratory muscle work.[5]

### Monitoring the PSV Patient

Because PSV is a pressure-assisted mode of ventilation, the patient is responsible for initiating all breaths. If the patient fatigues or is unable to generate an inspiratory effort, hypoventilation will result. For this reason, PSV is not used in patients with altered respiratory drive, poor pulmonary function, or compromised gas exchange. PSV can be combined with SIMV if a potential for hypoventilation exists.

Spontaneous ventilatory rate is a significant monitoring parameter during PSV. An increase in ventilatory rate to greater than 35 breaths per minute indicates respiratory muscle fatigue. Other clinical signs of muscle fatigue include abdominal paradox, respiratory alternans, and/or hypercapnia. General patient appearance and respiratory parameters such as tidal volume, minute ventilation, heart rate, and oxygen saturation should be documented. The recent generation of ventilators that incorporate this mode of ventilation include the Siemens Servo 900C, Puritan-Bennett 7200a, Bear 5, and Engstrom Erica.

### INVERSE RATIO VENTILATION

Inverse ratio ventilation (IRV) is a ventilatory support mode that results in an increased inspiratory time and a corresponding decrease in expiratory time. The normal inspiratory/expiratory (I:E) ratio is approximately 1:2. In IRV, the I:E ratio can be increased to 4:1. This is achieved by either slowing the inspiratory flow rate or by instituting a "hold" at the end of inspiration (Figure 4-3). Prolongation of the inspiratory phase allows greater time for alveoli to remain open and also lowers peak airway pressure, which occurs during other positive-pressure modes of ventilation. The shortened expiratory phase increases mean lung volume because the lungs are reinflated before complete expiration occurs. This leaves a higher residual volume in the lungs. Hence, a PEEP-like effect is created.

The mechanism by which PEEP improves oxygenation is well recognized. PEEP increases and maintains functional residual ca-

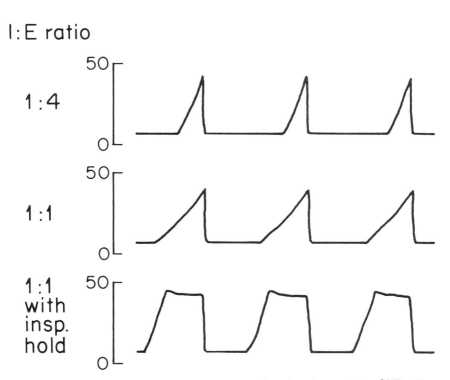

**Figure 4-3** Different airway pressure waves produced with a variety of I:E ratios and inspiratory hold.

pacity (FRC) of the lungs or lung volume at end expiration. By increasing FRC, previously collapsed alveoli are held open to allow for greater gas diffusion. The increase in mean lung volume that results from IRV is believed to achieve the same advantages as PEEP. For this reason, IRV is often referred to as auto-PEEP.

### Effects of IRV

Much of the data regarding physiological consequences of IRV come from animal studies. To date, few clinical trials using IRV have been reported. How oxygenation is improved during IRV continues to be debated. It has been postulated that prolonging inspiratory time can improve gas diffusion by the progressive recruitment and stabilization of previously collapsed alveolar units.[6] However, it may simply be the result of IRV's PEEP-like effect.

A study of nine patients receiving IRV (1.5:1) found significant improvement in oxygenation and compliance and a decrease in peak airway pressure compared with other ventilatory modes.[7] Improvement in oxygenation resulted from progressive recruitment of alveoli in performing gas exchange. Although increased peak airway pressure improves oxygenation, it increases the risk of pulmonary barotrauma. In IRV, improvement in oxygenation results at lower peak airway pressures.[6,7]

The suggestion that IRV improves oxygenation through its effect on mean airway pressure (mean pressure transmitted to the airways throughout both inspiration and expiration) remains disputed.[6,8] Oxygenation improved with a higher mean airway pressure.[9] An increase in mean airway pressure is commonly found in patients receiving IRV (4:1).[10] The increase in mean airway pressure was considerably lower than the level of PEEP that was necessary to produce the same end-expiratory volume. In this study, there was a reduction in pulmonary shunting and deadspace and an increase in carbon dioxide elimination.

IRV, as with PEEP, can have a deleterious effect on cardiac output. Mean airway pressure increases intrathoracic pressure. Venous return necessary for preload and maintenance of adequate cardiac output can be reduced by increasing intrathoracic pressure. Oxygen delivery, which is often compromised in acutely ill patients, could also be adversely affected by IRV. When compared with other ventilatory modes, IRV may increase oxygenation, but its effect may be negated if cardiac output and oxygen delivery are reduced. Because of IRV's PEEP-like effect, other potential adverse conditions that occur during PEEP may occur.

### Indications for IRV

Inverse ratio ventilation has been studied in infant and adult respiratory distress syndromes. In neonates with hyaline membrane disease, IRV improves oxygenation.[11] The increased I:E ratio (2:1) improved oxygenation at a lower fraction of inspired oxygen ($Fio_2$) and end-expiratory pressure. Adult respiratory distress syndrome refractory to conventional methods of mechanical ventilation also benefits from the application of IRV (up to 4:1).[6]

Maintenance of adequate oxygenation in patients with diffuse lung disease is often difficult. A longer inspiratory time may improve oxygenation by increasing the time that otherwise closed alveoli are kept open, allowing for greater gas diffusion. However, in other types of lung disease such as unilateral lung disease and chronic obstructive pulmonary disease, the longer inspiratory phase may result in overdistention of normal segments and air trapping with extreme hypercapnia. In the latter case, a longer expiratory time is needed for adequate elimination of carbon dioxide.

Application of IRV is usually reserved for patients with hypoxemia, diffuse lung injury, and failure to improve with conventional modes of mechanical ventilation. Relative hemodynamic stability is necessary since IRV may decrease cardiac output and oxygen delivery. Because IRV is an unnatural and uncomfortable mode of ventilation, patients require heavy sedation and frequently paralysis.

Although IRV resembles PEEP in terms of improving oxygenation, it may be more effective in lowering peak airway pressures, thus reducing the risk of barotrauma.[10] Whether a particular reversed I:E ratio can improve oxygenation without adversely affecting cardiac output and oxygen delivery is under investigation. An I:E ratio of less than 2:1 may achieve improved oxygenation without significantly affecting cardiac output.[10] As inspiratory time is decreased to a more normal I:E ratio, PEEP may need to be applied. By establishing a normal I:E ratio, a more complete exhalation of the tidal volume occurs, thus losing the auto-PEEP effect of IRV.

## Monitoring IRV Patients

Because of the complex effects of IRV on cardiac output and oxygen delivery, intensive monitoring is required. Monitoring parameters include

- hemodynamic measurements
- arterial blood gas determination
- oxygen saturation by continuous pulse oximetry
- tidal volume
- end-tidal carbon dioxide measurements ($PET_{CO_2}$)
- pressure and flow waveform analysis.

New generation ventilators have features that will plot waveform graphs that aid in monitoring IRV patients. The use of IRV requires well-trained personnel who understand the complex technology involved and potential adverse effects that may occur. To achieve IRV, the ventilator must be in the pressure control mode with appropriate adjustments of inspiratory time, PEEP, peak inspiratory pressure, ventilatory rate, and $Fio_2$.

PSV and IRV are new ventilatory modes that are just beginning to gain acceptance in clinical practice. More study and clinical experience are needed to further delineate their indications and usefulness.

## NEW GENERATION VENTILATORS

The latest generation of ventilators incorporates the use of microprocessors to control ventilator functions. These ventilators provide a variety of modes, functions, and monitoring capabilities. Examples of the new generation ventilators include the Bear 5, the Puritan-Bennett 7200a, and the Seimens Servo 900C. A discussion of the salient features of these ventilators follows. For specific information about one of these ventilators contact the following manufacturers:

- Bear Medical Systems, Inc.
  2085 Rustin Avenue
  Riverside, CA 92507

- Puritan-Bennett Corporation
  2310 Camino Vida Roble
  Carlsbad, CA 92009
- Siemens-Elema Ventilator Systems
  2360 North Palmer Drive
  Schaumburg, IL 60173–3887

## Bear 5

The Bear 5 ventilator is a microprocessor-controlled ventilator with a cathode ray tube (CRT) display monitor. The control panel is shown in Figure 4-4. The Bear 5 offers a comprehensive monitoring system and six modes of ventilation:

1. Continuous mandatory ventilation (CMV)
2. Assist CMV
3. SIMV/IMV
4. CPAP
5. Augmented minute ventilation (AMV)
6. Time-cycled ventilation

The Bear 5 also provides pressure support, capacity for IRV (up to 3:1), compliance compensation, and printer interface. The Bear 5 provides graphic display of proximal airway pressure, I:E volume, and I:E flow. Graphs can be "frozen" to allow for close examination. Also, graphs can be set to display two parameters (volume, flow, or airway pressure) simultaneously. The graphic display is also useful in detecting patient circuit leaks, patient disconnection, and possible air trapping.

In addition to the monitoring capabilities, the Bear 5 has a comprehensive alarm system. A convenient feature of this ventilator is the auto-set program when the ventilator automatically sets alarm parameters. When an alarm condition arises, an audible alarm is heard as well as visually displayed on the CRT and alarm indicator panel.

The AMV mode is a new function of the Bear 5 ventilator. AMV is a unique backup or weaning mode that is based on minute ventilation. It is a variable SIMV mode that supplements ventilation to achieve a minimum preset minute ventilation. For example, if a patient's average exhaled minute volume falls below the preset minimum, the ventilator assumes operation at a preset backup

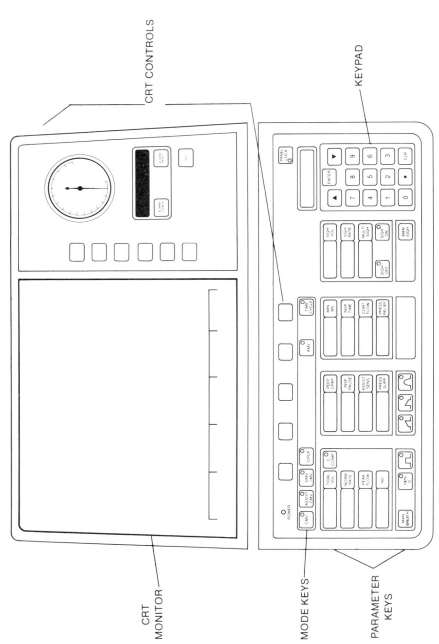

**Figure 4-4** Control panel of the Bear 5 Ventilator. *Source:* Courtesy of Bear Medical Systems Inc, Riverside, CA.

rate. The patient will still be able to breathe spontaneously, and mandatory breaths will be synchronized. AMV is also used in patients who have inconsistent minute volumes or who suffer from sleep apnea.

Compliance compensation is another feature of the Bear 5. This option calculates the deadspace volume in the ventilator circuitry and adjusts the tidal volume accordingly. The volume added to the preset tidal volume and that subtracted from the exhaled tidal volume are displayed on the CRT. Access to the various ventilatory modes of the Bear 5 is relatively simple. Once a mode is selected and the required and optional parameters are set, data are entered into the microprocessor. This puts the ventilator functionally into the mode selected.

## Puritan-Bennett 7200a

The Puritan-Bennett 7200a ventilator is an electronically powered, microprocessor-controlled volume ventilator. The microprocessor controls ventilator functions such as pneumatics (responsible for blending and delivering gas), monitoring of operational status, memory storage, alarms, and correction circuitry. Two solenoid valves are controlled by the microprocessor. These valves control volume of flow, $Fio_2$, and waveform of delivered gas. The ventilator is equipped with self-testing systems that include a power-on self-test and an extended self-test that checks the electronic and pneumatic functions. These self-test systems allow for detection of operational problems and activation of corrective measures. When a fault is detected, an alarm is activated and the ventilator assumes operation at a preprogrammed control ventilation mode (independent of the microprocessor) or opens a safety valve to allow the patient to breathe room air.

The Puritan-Bennett 7200a offers four operational modes (see control panel in Figure 4-5). These modes include CMV (allows assisted or controlled ventilation), SIMV, CPAP, and pressure support. PEEP is also provided. The ventilator is capable of delivering flow in three different waveforms: square, tapered, or sine wave.

One hundred percent oxygen is available for 2 minutes by pressing the 100% $O_2$ button, followed by pressing "Enter." After 2 minutes, the oxygen concentration returns to the previously set oxygen level. This option may be helpful following suctioning,

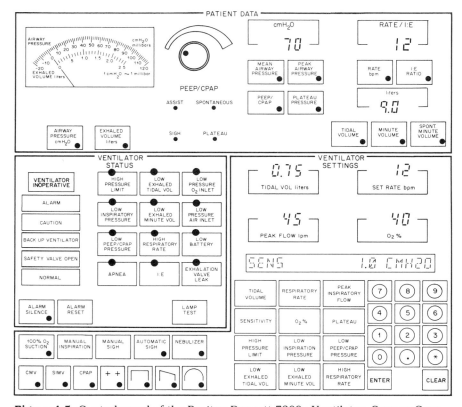

**Figure 4-5** Control panel of the Puritan-Bennett 7200a Ventilator. *Source:* Courtesy of Puritan-Bennett Corporation, Carlsbad, CA.

bronchoscopy, or other procedure-induced periods of hypoxemia. The 7200a can be customized to meet the needs for specific applications. One option, the 7202 display, adds a 18.6 × 30.5-cm electroluminescent amber monitor that is visible from a distance of 30 feet.

## Siemens Servo 900C

The Siemens Servo 900C is a pneumatically powered, electronically controlled ventilator. The control panel of this ventilator is

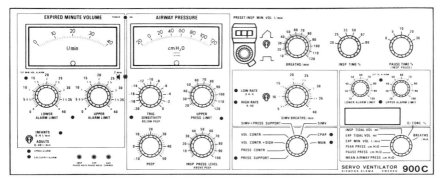

**Figure 4-6** Control panel of the Siemens Servo 900C Ventilator. *Source:* Courtesy of Siemens-Elema Ventilator Systems, Schaumburg, IL.

shown in Figure 4-6. The Servo 900C can operate in eight different modes:

1. Volume controlled
2. Volume controlled + sigh
3. Pressure controlled
4. Pressure support
5. SIMV
6. SIMV + pressure support
7. CPAP
8. Manual

The 900C also has the capability of providing IRV up to 4:1. As with previous models of the Servo 900 series, tidal volume is not set as such in this volume ventilator. A minimum minute volume and ventilatory rate are set. The average tidal volume is equal to the minimum minute volume divided by the ventilatory rate. Additionally, inspiratory time as a percentage of the respiratory cycle is set. Inspiratory pause time as a percentage of the respiratory cycle may also be set. A variety of optional oxygen and carbon dioxide monitors are also available.

**REFERENCES**

1. MacIntyre NR: Pressure support ventilation: Effects on ventilatory reflexes and ventilatory-muscle workloads. *Respir Care* 1987;32:447–453.

2. Brochard L, Pluskwa F, Lemaire F: Improved efficacy of spontaneous breathing with inspiratory pressure support. *Am Rev Respir Dis* 1987;136:411–415.

3. Prakash O, Meij S: Cardiopulmonary response to inspiratory pressure support during spontaneous ventilation vs. conventional ventilation. *Chest* 1985;88:403–407.

4. Murphy DF, Dobb GD: Effect of pressure support on spontaneous breathing during intermittent mandatory ventilation. *Crit Care Med* 1987;15:612–613.

5. Fahey PJ, Vanderwarf C, David A: A comparison of oxygen costs of breathing during weaning with continuous positive airway pressure versus pressure support ventilation. *Am Rev Respir Dis* 1985;131:A130.

6. Gurevitch MJ, Van Dyke J, Young ES, Jackson K: Improved oxygenation and lower peak airway pressure in severe adult respiratory distress syndrome: Treatment with inverse ratio ventilation. *Chest* 1986;89:211–213.

7. Ravizza AG, et al: Inverse ratio and conventional ventilation: Comparison of respiratory effects. *Anesthesiology* 1983;59:A523.

8. Berman LS, Downs JB, Van Eeden A, Delhagen D: Inspiration:expiration ratio: Is mean airway pressure the difference? *Crit Care Med* 1981;9:775–777.

9. Boros SJ: Variations in inspiratory:expiratory ratio and airway pressure waveform during mechanical ventilation: Significance of mean airway pressure. *J Pediatr* 1979;94:114–117.

10. Cole AG, Weller SF, Sykes MK: Inverse ratio ventilation compared with PEEP in adult respiratory failure. *Intensive Care Med* 1984;10:227–232.

11. Spahr RC, Klein AM, Brown DR, MacDonald HM, Holzman IR: Hyaline membrane disease: A controlled study of inspiratory to expiratory ratio in its management by ventilator. *Am J Dis Child* 1980;134:373–376.

**RECOMMENDED READING**

Delafosse B, Bouffard Y, Viale JP, Annat G, Bertrand O, Motin J: Respiratory changes induced by parenteral nutrition in postoperative patients undergoing inspiratory pressure support ventilation. *Anesthesiology* 1987;66:393–396.

Dupuis YG: *Ventilators: Theory and Clinical Application.* St. Louis, CV Mosby Co, 1986.

Esbenshade J: Pressure support ventilation. *Crit Care Med* 1986;14:665–666.

Kanak R, Fahey PJ, Vanderwarf C: Oxygen cost of breathing: Changes dependent upon mode of mechanical ventilation. *Chest* 1985;87:126–127.

MacIntyre NR: Respiratory function during pressure support ventilation. *Chest* 1986;89:677–683.

Perel A: Using pressure support in a rational way. *Chest* 1987;91:153–154.

Pinsky MR, Summer WR: Cardiac augmentation by phasic high intrathoracic pressure support in man. *Chest* 1983;84:370–375.

# Pulse Oximetry

*Susan Joy Nelson*

# 5

Oxygen supply is essential for maintenance of life. Functional hemoglobin, contained in red blood cells, is the primary transport mechanism of oxygen. Approximately 97% of the oxygen is carried by hemoglobin, as oxyhemoglobin, by arteries to body tissue.[1] Disease, injury, drugs, and procedures can alter the oxygen-carrying capacity of the blood and interfere with the supply of oxygen to the tissues. Consequently, it is important to monitor the arterial oxygen saturation.

It is common practice for clinicians to evaluate the skin, nail beds, and oral mucosa for cyanosis in an effort to determine the adequacy of oxygenation. In 1947, Comroe and associates demonstrated that, with good lighting and adequate hemoglobin concentration, cyanosis could be detected only when 15% of the hemoglobin was desaturated.[2] In addition, when the hemoglobin level was below normal, as in anemia, cyanosis was more difficult to detect. Physical assessment provides a rough and potentially inaccurate estimate of oxygenation. Arterial blood gas (ABG) analysis provides an accurate assessment of oxygen saturation, but it is an invasive, intermittent, and costly procedure. ABG analysis often requires a turnaround time that exceeds that desired in the clinical situation. Pulse oximetry can provide oxygen saturation monitoring on a continuous or intermittent basis, without delay, with minimal discomfort to the patient. Pulse oximetry can also provide early warning of hypoxemia, which facilitates intervention prior to the development of complications.[3-5]

## PRINCIPLES

A major challenge in developing oximetry into a practical tool for clinical use was differentiating between the light absorption of oxy-

53

genated hemoglobin, unoxygenated hemoglobin, and other body tissues. In 1975, Nakajima and associates reported that the rhythmic variation in arterial volume could be used as a signal to make the necessary differentiation.[2] Arterial volume variations and the Lambert-Beer law of light absorbance allow measurement of arterial saturation noninvasively. The Lambert-Beer law states that the absorbance of light by a substance is directly proportional to the ability of that substance to absorb light and the concentration of the substance.[2] Skin, bone, muscle, and fluid absorb a constant amount of light whereas arterial blood absorbs varying amounts of light.[3]

Each blood constituent absorbs a different amount of light. In addition, the various blood components absorb light differently in each light spectrum. Oxygenated and unoxygenated hemoglobin show no difference at the red band with a wavelength of 800 nm. Oxyhemoglobin has a significant increase in light absorption in the red band spectrum from 600 to 750 nm. Compared with oxyhemoglobin, however, hemoglobin absorbs half of the amount of light in the red band of wavelength 900 to 1,000 nm. Carboxyhemoglobin is transparent to infrared light, and infrared light is not absorbed to a measurable degree by oxygen. These characteristics allow the measurement of functional hemoglobin concentration. The density change of arterial blood is the result of the rhythmic distention of arterioles as blood is ejected by the heart.[3] The rhythmic arteriolar pulsation provides the operational signal for pulse oximetry.

The transducer of a pulse oximeter contains two light-emitting diodes (LEDs) and a photodiode.[5] The LEDs generate the constant visible red wavelength of light at 660 nm and an infrared wavelength of light at 940 nm.[5,6] The photodiode detects the red and infrared light transmitted through the tissues and blood.[2,6] A block diagram of a pulse oximeter and transducer is shown in Figure 5-1. The pulsatile light received by the photodiode is due to arterial pulsation, which causes varying amounts of light to be absorbed by the blood as arteriolar distention changes.[3] Based on the light absorption properties of oxygenated and unoxygenated hemoglobin at these two wavelengths, the oximeter processes the signal received by the photodiode to determine the oxygen saturation of arterial blood.[2,3,7] A typical signal received by the photodiode and sent for processing is diagrammed in Figure 5-2.[7]

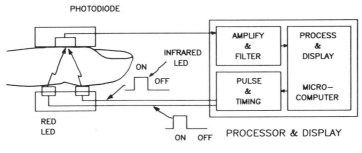

PHOTODIODE

INFRARED
LED

AMPLIFY
&
FILTER

PROCESS
&
DISPLAY

ON

OFF

PULSE
&
TIMING

MICRO-
COMPUTER

RED
LED

ON    OFF    PROCESSOR & DISPLAY

TRANSDUCER

**Figure 5-1** Block diagram of a pulse oximeter showing the transducer positioned on the finger, the light-emitting diodes (LEDs), and the photodiode sensor. Each LED generates a constant wavelength of light, and the photodiode receives the non-absorbed light. The information is sent from the photodiode to the microcomputer and then processed and displayed. *Source:* Reprinted from *Journal of Cardiovascular Nursing* (1987;1[3]:81), Copyright © 1987, Aspen Publishers Inc.

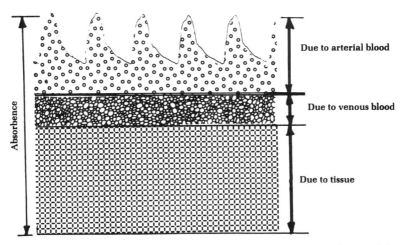

Due to arterial blood

Due to venous blood

Due to tissue

Absorbence

**Figure 5-2** The light received by the photodiode appears as a pulsatile signal due to the rhythmic distention of the arteriole as blood pulses through. The diagram represents pulsatile signal variations in absorption of light superimposed over nonspecific absorption signals of other tissue and fluid. *Source:* Reprinted from *Journal of Cardiovascular Nursing* (1987;1[3]:82), Copyright © 1987, Aspen Publishers Inc.

Dual-signal pulse oximeters (e.g., Nellcor N-200) use the previously described sensor to detect pulse as the operational signal. In addition, these oximeters use the electrocardiogram (ECG) to differentiate between artifact and pulsatile flow. When using the ECG synchronization mode, the microprocessor opens a window of approximately 200 msec following each R wave on the ECG. Obtaining saturation during this period reduces motion artifact caused by patient movement or intra-aortic balloon counterpulsation. It is also possible to obtain accurate saturation determinations in patients with low perfusion states.

## CLINICAL APPLICATION

Pulse oximeters may be used intermittently or continuously for oxygen saturation monitoring. Most pulse oximeters are designed primarily for either continuous monitoring on a single patient or intermittent use on multiple patients. The variability in patient situations makes the availability of these two types of oximeter desirable.

Suboptimal oxygenation is associated with symptoms that are not exclusively signs of hypoxemia. Patients who demonstrate symptoms of restlessness, confusion, dysrhythmias, fever, or shortness of breath can be assessed quickly using a portable oximeter designed for intermittent use. Patients recovering from surgery or those on strict bed rest are prone to pulmonary complications such as atelectasis, airway secretion accumulation, and ineffective breathing related to sedation. Pulse oximeters allow for quick and continuous assessment of the need for pulmonary toilet. In patients requiring frequent suctioning or aggressive respiratory care, the pulse oximeter provides a method of evaluating the effectiveness of treatment without frequent, invasive arterial blood gas analysis. At the onset of acute symptoms or in the arrest situation, intermittent oxygen saturation offers an immediate assessment of oxygenation while ABG analysis is pending.

Continuous pulse oximetry has many clinical applications. Patients with oxygenation or circulation problems would benefit from noninvasive, continuous monitoring of oxygen saturation. Patients on ventilators can receive continuous monitoring of oxygen saturation. Adjustment of ventilator parameters can be made in a more timely manner than with ABG analysis. In addition, patients can often be weaned from a ventilator more quickly and with less ABG sampling. In the operating room, continuous pulse oximetry provides an additional assessment component of effective ventilation and an early warning before patient decompensation ensues. Pulse oximetry provides a backup warning system for equipment failure, such as ventilators or oxygen delivery equipment.[8] One of the primary concerns in the postanesthesia recovery unit is the adequacy of the patient's airway and breathing. With continuous oxygen saturation readings, staff do not need to speculate on whether slow or shallow respirations are providing adequate oxygenation. Continuous monitoring during tracheal suctioning allows timely completion of the procedure before saturation falls to compromising levels. Continuous pulse oximetry is also used to evaluate sleep apnea.

Pulse oximetry provides a rapid and accurate assessment of oxygenation. It can help reduce costs by reducing the number of ABG samples, by reducing infections from frequent access of indwelling arterial lines, and by allowing staff to use their time more effectively because of the immediacy of results.

## CLINICAL OPERATION

Portable pulse oximeters are intended for intermittent observation of oxygen saturation. These units operate on rechargeable batteries and provide a printed record of date, time, heart rate, and oxygen saturation or a graphic display of saturation over time. The sensor/transducer for these units is not disposable. Units designed for intermittent use require an average of ten pulses to obtain a reading.

Most pulse oximeters for continuous single patient monitoring use an electrical power source. They have battery backup that allows these units to operate 1 to 2 hours during transport and power outages.[9] Most models show a pulse signal in the form of a bouncing light bar or a pulse waveform. Display of the pulse signal is necessary for assessing the signal quality for artifact. These units contain adjustable audible alarm systems for high and low pulse rate and for high and low oxygen saturation. Each has default alarm limits that operate until the user sets patient-specific limits. The display indicates when the unit is operating on backup battery power. Unit calibration is not required due to design characteristics.[2,3,7]

## DISPLAY SCREEN

Two types of displays are commonly used in pulse oximeters for continuous single-patient monitoring. They are light-emitting diode (LED) and liquid crystal display (LCD) displays. The LED display usually has red figures on a nonreflective black background, which is easily read from a distance of 6 to 12 feet from any angle. The LED display is clearly visible in total darkness as well as in lighted areas.

The LCD screen has black figures on a silvery/gold background. LCD units are on a tilt base to allow adjustment when light reflection obscures the readout. However, the unit will need adjustment of the tilt or viewing angle whenever the observer changes position. Many LCD screens have a backlit screen to improve readability in a dark environment. Most pulse oximeters designed for intermittent multiple patient use have LCD screens. The LED display is easier to read at greater distances than the LCD screen. A comparison of features of the two types of displays is provided in Table 5-1.

## SENSOR

The low intensity light generated by the transducer's LEDs requires application of the sensor to an area of thin tissue.[3] This will allow the light to be transmitted through the tissue without total absorbance. Sites commonly used are the bridge of the nose, fingers and toes, webbing between digits, and ear lobes. In neonates, hands and feet may also be used. There are a variety of disposable and nondisposable sensors available. The choice of sensor depends on the monitoring site, age of the patient, and estimated length of monitoring. Several of the sensors available are shown in Figure 5-3.

During application of the Band-aid–like probe, the LED must be positioned directly opposite the light-sensing photodiode.[9] This enables the oximeter to detect the pulse, which signals the processor to determine oxygen saturation. Proper placement can be verified by comparing the patient's pulse rate to the oximeter's pulse rate

**Table 5-1** Summary of LED and LCD Displays

| Characteristic | LED | LCD |
|---|---|---|
| Display visibility | Excellent | Good; reflection obscures readings; screen is adjustable |
| Visible distance | 12 feet or greater; red figures visible over greater distance | 7 feet maximum; black figures are not visible at distances of more than several feet |
| Visibility in darkness | Excellent | Moderately good; darkness obliterates the black figures unless the background is lighted |
| Pulse signal quality | Yes, bouncing LED light bar | Some models, LCD waveform |
| Battery life | 1 hour | 1 hour plus |
| Dual signal models | 2 hours | |
| Battery life on full recharge | 8 hours | 8 hours |
| Dual signal models | 14 hours | |

display. Within a few pulsations, usually five to seven, the oxygen saturation will be displayed continuously and updated on a pulse-to-pulse basis.

## POTENTIAL PROBLEMS

Movement, strong ambient light, long or artificial fingernails, and dark skin may interfere with pulse detection. Movement causes the pulse display to exceed the actual heart rate, and loss of signal may occur. Immobilization of the extremity or use of an ECG synchronized pulse oximeter will improve signal quality, while decreasing artifact and false alarms. Strong ambient light will prevent the photodiode from recognizing light transmitted through the tissues and result in signal loss. Covering the probe with a towel or foil will correct this problem. Long fingernails may prevent proper alignment of the sensor and light-emitting windows.[9] Artificial nails may obstruct transmission of light through the finger. In either case, selection of an alternate monitoring site would

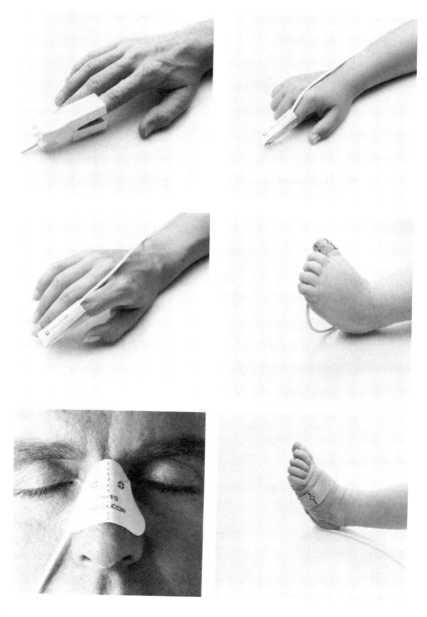

**Figure 5-3** An assortment of pulse oximeter sensors are available for use in various sites on patients of various sizes. *Source:* Courtesy of Nellcor, Hayward, CA.

be appropriate. Additional information about potential causes of oximeter malfunction and the interventions appropriate to correct the difficulties is presented in Table 5-2.[10] The monitoring cable that attaches the sensor to the oximeter is made of fiberglass, which may break if it is bent. The cable should be coiled loosely for storage.

In the critical care area, it is not uncommon to encounter patients with circulatory problems as a result of vasoactive drugs, hypotension, hypothermia, or disease processes. Decreased peripheral perfusion from any cause can decrease the usefulness of the pulse oximeter since it relies on arterial pulsation as a trigger.[5] In cases in which impaired circulation may affect readings, it is best to apply the pulse oximeter to an ear lobe or bridge of the nose, since these areas tend to vasoconstrict later. Pulse oximeters that have the ECG synchronization feature may be more accurate in low perfusion states since the sensing window is triggered by the R wave.

## PATIENT CARE CONSIDERATIONS

The LEDs do not generate heat. Therefore, there is no risk of burns nor need for frequent site rotation.[3] The plastic adhesive tape on the disposable probes may cause skin irritation.[9] Site inspection should be made every 8 hours, and site rotation should decrease any irritation. The plastic tape may be removed and replaced with hypoallergenic tape in severely allergic patients. The nondisposable probes do not use tape and may be the most appropriate for allergic patients.

The electrical components of the probes are isolated from the environment. Damaged probes or probes with exposed wires should not be used. Neither the probe nor cable should be immersed in liquid.

Some pulse oximeters have a 12-foot cable that allows patients to turn and be out of bed in a chair while monitored. Others provide an extension cable for the patient probe.

## ACCURACY

Pulse oximeters of the late 1970s and early 1980s overestimated oxygen saturation.[2] Readings of 70% occurred by oximetry when

**Table 5-2** Troubleshooting Problems with Pulse Oximeters

| Signal Interference | Cause | Intervention |
|---|---|---|
| Pulse rate display exceeds actual heart rate. | Bright light in environment (i.e., phototherapy, heat lamps, and sunlight) | • Cover sensor with towel or sheet.<br>• Cover sensor with foil. |
| | Motion artifact from probe slipping | • Use adhesive sensor.<br>• Immobilize extremity.<br>• Select less mobile site.<br>• Use ECG synchronization feature. |
| | Electrocautery device | • Plug cautery device into a separate AC circuit.<br>• Move ground pad as close to the surgical site as possible.<br>• Move sensor site as far from ground pad as possible.<br>• Move the pulse oximeter as far as possible from the electrocautery unit. |
| Pulse rate display is less than actual heart rate. | Cardiac arrest without cardiopulmonary resuscitation | • Initiate cardiopulmonary resuscitation, counterpulsation. |
| | Blood pressure cuff inflated proximal to sensor, intra-aortic balloon has advanced, or arterial line has reduced distal flow | • Move sensor or blood pressure cuff to another extremity. |
| | Intense vasoconstriction from drugs, hypothermia, hypovolemia, and hypotension | • Change sensor to nasal site.<br>• Use ECG synchronization feature. |
| | Sensor unplugged from unit | • Plug sensor into unit.<br>• Turn unit on. |
| | Artificial fingernail | • Select alternate sensor site. |
| | Optical windows of sensor misaligned | • Reapply sensor. |
| | Sensor applied too tightly | • Reapply sensor. |
| | Severe anemia or hemodilution (Hgb < 5 g/dl) | • Transfuse with packed red blood cells. |
| | Patient cable sharply bent (fiberoptic filaments may be broken) | • Straighten cable.<br>• Replace cable. |

**Table 5-2** *continued*

| Signal Interference | Cause | Intervention |
|---|---|---|
| Signal is lost or there is double counting of pulse rate. | Pulsatile venous pressure (e.g., severe right-sided heart failure, tricuspid regurgitation, increased intrathoracic pressures, and obstructed venous return) | • Elevate sensor site above heart level.<br>• Reduce ventilator pressures.<br>• Use ECG synchronization feature. |
| Saturation display is inaccurate. | Cardiogreen and other intravascular dyes depending on concentration | • Compare result with saturation obtained by arterial blood gas analysis.<br>• Wait for dye levels to decrease. |
| | Carboxyhemoglobin and other dyshemoglobins if present in sufficient quantities (e.g., smoke or exhaust inhalation) | • Obtain blood specimen for arterial blood gas determination. |
| Display is blank. | Unit turned off or battery uncharged | • Turn unit on.<br>• Plug into AC power source.<br>• Recharge battery of portable unit. |
| Machine functions on AC power, but BATT IN USE indicator is always lit. | Power base disconnected from unit | • Reconnect unit to power base. |
| | Power cord | • Connect power cord to unit.<br>• Connect power cord to another AC outlet.<br>• Replace power cord. |
| | AC fuse defective | • Replace fuse on rear panel. |
| Patient sensor cannot be connected to cable. | Bent connector pins | • Carefully straighten pins.<br>• Replace the sensor. |
| | Incorrect sensor for type of pulse oximeter in use | • Replace the sensor with correct one for the unit. |

*Source:* Adapted with permission from *Journal of Clinical Monitoring* (1985;1[2]:126–129), Copyright ©1985, Little, Brown & Company.

the actual saturation was 50%.[2,11] All subsequent oximeters use empiric algorithms to correct the overestimation problems.[2]

The accuracy of the new-generation pulse oximeters has been confirmed through laboratory and clinical trials.[12-14] For example, Mihm and Halperin evaluated finger pulse oximetry using a Nellcor unit on patients with respiratory distress and respiratory failure.[5] Their findings showed excellent correlation between the pulse oximeter and arterial blood samples for saturation levels from 65% to 100%. Use of the pulse oximeter allowed identification of life-threatening episodes (with saturation < 70%) before clinical symptoms were present. Additionally, the pulse oximeter functioned properly on patients with hypotension and those receiving intravenous infusion of vasoactive medications at doses below the alpha range. Additional studies confirmed the accuracy of pulse oximetry over an arterial oxygen saturation range from 63% to 100% in healthy adults[6] and neonates.[3]

## CASE STUDIES

Three cases, drawn from clinical practice situations, are briefly presented to demonstrate the usefulness of pulse oximetry in assessing patients and evaluating interventions.

### Case 1

Following surgical repair of tetralogy of Fallot, a 3-month old, 5-kg boy was admitted to the cardiac surgical intensive care unit. Monitors included the electrocardiogram, right and left atrial pressures, right radial arterial pressure, rectal and toe temperatures, and a pulse oximeter. An oral, uncuffed endotracheal tube was intact with symmetrical chest rise and audible bilateral breath sounds. The patient was placed on a pressure-cycled ventilator. Heat lamp therapy was initiated for a rectal temperature of 35°C (95°F). There were no responses to stimulation due to the continued effects of anesthesia. Admission proceeded uneventfully until the arterial oxygen saturation ($Sa_{O_2}$), measured by pulse oximetry, dropped suddenly. In 30 seconds, the saturation dropped from 100% to 80%. There were no changes in heart rate, skin color, lung compliance, or heart and lung sounds.

Endotracheal suctioning failed to produce any effect. The endotracheal tube was removed, and the infant was immediately reintubated with a new endotracheal tube. These actions resulted in a rapid increase in the $Sao_2$ to 100%. The original endotracheal tube was completely obstructed with thick secretions.

Continuous monitoring of oxygen saturation by pulse oximetry allowed quick detection of hypoxemia and correction of the underlying cause before circulatory collapse could occur. It is important to note that the pulse oximeter was accurate and reliable in a clinical situation in which the infant was hypothermic and in an area of bright light.

### Case 2

A 45-year-old man with cardiomyopathy underwent four-vessel aortocoronary arterial bypass surgery. Continuous pulse oximetry was used to assess oxygen saturation during weaning from mechanical ventilation. Arterial blood and mixed venous blood gases were obtained every 4 hours to assess the adequacy of cardiac output and metabolic state. The oxygen saturation by pulse oximetry was noted and recorded with each arterial blood gas analysis. The values obtained by both methods were identical despite the use of multiple vasoactive intravenous medications (dobutamine, 5.6 $\mu$g/kg/min; dopamine, 10.2 $\mu$g/kg/min; epinephrine, 0.11 $\mu$g/kg/min; nitroglycerin, 0.25 $\mu$g/kg/min) and mechanical cardiac assistance with an intra-aortic balloon (systolic, 70 mm Hg; diastolic, 40 mm Hg; augmented diastolic, 90 mm Hg). The patient was successfully weaned from mechanical ventilation and extubated on the second postoperative day. Continuous pulse oximetry was performed during his ICU stay to assess the effectiveness of pulmonary hygiene measures.

During this patient's postoperative course, there were periods of hypotension. Neither hypotension nor the vasoactive drugs interfered with obtaining an adequate pulse signal for the oximeter using the middle finger of the left hand.

## Case 3

A 58-year-old man was admitted to the medical intensive care unit with respiratory failure requiring intubation and mechanical ventilation. The ventilator settings were:

| | |
|---|---|
| $Fio_2$ | 0.60 |
| Tidal volume | 750 ml |
| Mode | assist/control |
| Rate | 14 |
| PEEP | 5 cm $H_2O$ |

He had several periods of restlessness and confusion with a stable oxygen saturation during the first 3 days. On the fourth day, the pulse oximeter showed a rapid drop in saturation from 92% to 80%, accompanied by an increase in heart rate from 86 to 141, restlessness, and decreased breath sounds on the right side. The physician performed a needle thoracostomy of the right chest, which resulted in an immediate improvement in oxygen saturation. A chest tube was placed and relieved the remaining pneumothorax. Pulse oximetry alerted the nurse and physician, resulting in rapid assessment, diagnosis, and treatment of a potentially life-threatening problem. Arterial blood gas analysis and chest radiography would not have permitted timely assessment to prevent further decompensation in this patient.

## SUMMARY

Clinical indicators of hypoxemia vary between patients in severity and in time of onset in relation to compromise. Continuous pulse oximetry aids early recognition of impending problems. Early recognition permits earlier diagnosis and treatment. Patients who require monitoring of arterial blood gases, mechanical ventilation, or frequent pulmonary care benefit from pulse oximetry. It is less costly than arterial blood gas analysis, more accurate than visual assessment,[2] equally accurate with oxygen saturation obtained by blood gas analysis,[3,5,6] and more time efficient. Pulse oximetry cannot, however, replace blood gas analysis for determining pH or $Paco_2$. Several manufacturers, however, have introduced hybrid monitors that have pulse oximetry functions and capnography (end-tidal carbon dioxide) capabilities. These monitors will prove useful in those institutions that do not have capnography capabilities.

## REFERENCES

1. Guyton AC: *Textbook of Medical Physiology.* Philadelphia, WB Saunders Co, 1981.

2. Severinghaus JW, Astrup PB: History of blood gas analysis: IV. Oximetry. *J Clin Monit* 1986;2:270–288.

3. Deckardt R, Steward DJ: Noninvasive arterial hemoglobin oxygen saturation versus transcutaneous oxygen tension monitoring in the preterm infant. *Crit Care Med* 1984;12:935–939.

4. Brooks TD, Gravenstein N: Pulse oximetry for early detection of hypoxemia in anesthetized infants. *J Clin Monit* 1984;1:135–137.

5. Mihm F, Halperin B. Noninvasive detection of profound arterial desaturation using a pulse oximetry device. *Anesthesiology* 1985;62:85–87.

6. Yelderman M, New W: Evaluation of pulse oximetry. *Anesthesiology* 1983;59:349–352.

7. Gardner R: Pulse oximetry. Monitoring's silver bullet. *J Cardiovasc Nurs* 1987;1:79–83.

8. Cooper JB, Newbower RS, Kitz RJ: An analysis of major errors and equipment failures in anesthesia management: Considerations for prevention and detection. *Anesthesiology* 1984;60:34–42.

9. Nellcor Incorporated: *Non-Invasive Arterial Oxygen Monitoring.* Hayward, CA, Nellcor, 1987.

10. New W: Pulse oximetry. *J Clin Monit* 1984;1:126–129.

11. Chapman KR, Liu FLW, Warson RM, Rebuck AS: Range of accuracy of two wavelength oximetry. *Chest* 1986;89:540–542.

12. Boxer RA, Gottesfeld I, Singh S, LaCorte MA, Parnell VA, Walker P: Noninvasive pulse oximetry in children with cyanotic congenital heart disease. *Crit Care Med* 1987;15:1062–1064.

13. Sendak MJ, Harris AP, Donham RT: Use of pulse oximetry to assess arterial oxygen saturation during newborn resuscitation. *Crit Care Med* 1986;14:739–740.

14. Taylor MB, Whitwam JG: The current status of pulse oximetry: Clinical value of continuous noninvasive oxygen saturation monitoring. *Anaesthesia* 1986;41:943–949.

### RECOMMENDED READING

Barker SJ, Tremper KK: Pulse oximetry: Applications and limitations. *Int Anesth Clin* 1987;25(3):155–175.

Cecil WT, Thorpe KJ, Fibuch EE, Tuohy GF: A clinical evaluation of the accuracy of the Nellcor N-100 and Ohmeda 3700 pulse oximeters. *J Clin Monit* 1988;4:31–36.

Cohen DE, Downes JJ, Raphaely RC: What difference does pulse oximetry make? *Anesthesiology* 1988;67:181–183.

Huch A: Limitations of pulse oximetry. *Lancet* 1988;1(Feb 13):357.

King T, Simon RH: Pulse oximetry for tapering supplemental oxygen in hospitalized patients: Evaluation of a protocol. *Chest* 1987;92:713–716.

Mendelson Y, Kent JC, Shahnarian A, Welch GW, Giasi RM: Evaluation of the Datascope Accusat pulse oximeter in healthy adults. *J Clin Monit* 1988;4:59–63.

Pologe JA: Pulse oximetry: Technical aspects of machine design. *Int Anesth Clin* 1987;25(3):137–153.

Ridley SA: A comparison of two pulse oximeters: Assessment of accuracy at low arterial saturation in paediatric surgical patients. *Anaesthesia* 1988;43:136–140.

Warley ARH, Mitchell JH, Stradling JR: Evaluation of the Ohmeda 3700 pulse oximeter. *Thorax* 1987;42:892–896.

# Noninvasive Cardiac Output Determination

*Mary Woo*

# 6

Cardiac output is an important key to a person's cardiovascular condition. This becomes particularly important in patients with myocardial dysfunction and fluid overload because cardiac output is a reflection of actual cardiac performance and is a product of stroke volume and heart rate. Cardiac output is defined as the amount of blood ejected into the systemic circulation per unit time (usually expressed in liters of blood per minute). All of the available procedures to determine cardiac output can be divided into invasive and noninvasive methods.

The most common method to measure cardiac output is with a thermodilution catheter, which is an invasive technique. Thermodilution measures cardiac output by the injection of a solution of known quantity and temperature into the right atrium. The change in pulmonary artery blood temperature over time that results from the introduction of this fluid is measured by a thermistor located 4 cm from the catheter tip. This information is used by the attached cardiac output computer to calculate the cardiac output. Because this technique is invasive, it involves risks of infection, pain, air embolus or thromboembolus, dysrhythmia, or death. In addition to these risks, the thermodilution technique is expensive and requires skilled operators (for its insertion and operation), active operator involvement during data collection, intermittent availability of information, and admission of the patient to the ICU. There are multiple potential sources of error in its use. For example, patient respiratory variation, patient temperature, volume of injectate, temperature of injectate, ambient temperature, equipment malfunctions, and the proficiency of the person using the device may all possibly contribute to erroneous results when using the thermodilution method.[1] Under ideal conditions and technique there is an estimated biologic error in thermodilution results of from 15% to 20%.[2]

After this short review of the multiple problems associated with the most popular invasive method of measuring cardiac outputs, one can readily understand the need for the discovery of an accurate, noninvasive procedure. For clinicians, the ideal cardiac output measurement device would have the following characteristics:

- noninvasive
- high correlation with Fick or thermodilution methods
- high patient acceptance/comfort
- minimal skill/training requirements for operation
- minimal operator involvement required for collection of information
- potential for continuous measurement
- rapid data access
- reproducible results
- functionally accurate in a wide variety of patient populations
- low cost per patient

Many currently available, popular, noninvasive methods, such as blood pressure measurement sphygmomanometry, electrocardiography, and determination of heart rate are of little diagnostic help in early cardiac dysfunction. In the search for better noninvasive measures, two techniques, Doppler and transthoracic bioimpedance, have been developed to measure cardiac output.

## DOPPLER TECHNOLOGY

Doppler technology has been used for years in noninvasive procedures to measure such physiological aspects as peripheral blood pressures and patency of blood vessels such as the carotid arteries and deep veins. The Doppler technique is based on the concept (Doppler principle) that when a constant magnitude of ultrasonic waves is aimed at moving objects (in this case, red blood cells) the resultant reflection (backscatter) of those waves off the red blood cells causes the returning frequency to be altered proportionately to the velocity of the blood flow. It is this difference in frequency between the emitted and the then later received Doppler ultrasound waves that results in a frequency shift. The velocity of the blood flow can be calculated from the resulting shift in the magnitude and direction of the frequency.

Doppler echocardiographic assessment of cardiac output is based on the velocity of blood flow through the ascending aorta. It assumes that the main current of blood occurs in a direction parallel to the walls of the aorta. This technique is also dependent on the ability of the Doppler device to examine a cross-sectional area of this vessel in a Doppler pulse wave position perpendicular to the aorta's walls during an ejection interval of the heart.

There are generally two different procedures involved in measuring cardiac output using a Doppler device. The procedure to be used will depend on the clinical setting of the patient. One method requires the internal placement of a small Doppler probe in the esophagus at the level of the ascending aorta. It is used solely during surgical procedures, when the patient is unconscious. In order to "aim" this esophageal probe at the appropriate area of the ascending aorta, the operator would have to compare results using it to those of an externally placed Doppler probe. The esophageal probe would be turned or repositioned until the cardiac output recordings closely approximated the values obtained with the external Doppler probe. Minimal patient risk and the availability of continuous cardiac output measurements are advantages of this technique. On the other hand, its dependence on the success of the external Doppler probe for determination of correct esophageal position as well as its potential for extreme patient discomfort limits its use outside of surgery.

The second Doppler technique involves the external placement of a Doppler probe on the chest and then angling the probe toward the ascending aorta. There are three major sites for this probe head placement, which are also known as sonic windows. The most frequent sonic window used is at the suprasternal notch, but alternate sites such as the right and left supraclavicular areas have been used with success when sternal notch placement is not possible.

The multiple assumptions inherent in the theory of Doppler cardiac output determination and the importance of correct technique can cause problems and introduce inaccuracies into the values obtained. For example, the aorta is asymmetrical and does not maintain a continuous diameter throughout its length. The aortic walls cannot be considered to be strictly parallel. As a result, the correct positioning of the beam from the Doppler probe head may be difficult to achieve. Another example of potential error is overestimation of the aortic cross-sectional area. A large overestimation of the cross-sectional area would result in an overestimation of the cardiac output, and, conversely, the underestimation of the area could give a lower than actual cardiac output. Even small errors in the estimation of aortic diameter can result in significantly inaccurate cardiac output measurements. Additionally, turbulent blood flow, in conditions such as anemia, fever, or sepsis, may also introduce measurement error. There is also some controversy about what segment of the aorta should be used as the target for the Doppler beam or for aortic diameter determination. Although several studies have used varying portions of the ascending aorta with success, others have found that the use of any aortic section other than the orifice of the aortic valve could lead to significant (50%–100%) overestimation of stroke volume and thus of cardiac output.[3,4]

Although there have been no reported notable deleterious effects of Doppler ultrasonic waves on the adult human, there are definite drawbacks to its use. The suprasternal notch placement site for the probe head cannot be used in subjects with a tracheostomy, and extensive neck or chest dressings may preclude the use of the supraclavicular positions as well. Even if dressings do not completely cover the sonic window sites, the use of the Doppler probe head as well as the Doppler conduction gel has the potential for infecting any nearby open wound.

Perhaps an even greater drawback to the Doppler technique is the fact that currently available machines require a great deal of technical expertise and operating time. Even under expert guidance, the use of the Doppler probe head in obtaining an estimate of cardiac output can consume as much as 10 to 45 minutes for each data collection interval. What is particularly discouraging is the fact that even after finally obtaining an acceptable reading with the Doppler apparatus, the entire process must begin anew each time information regarding cardiac output is required. This is because the cardiac data obtained with this method (with the exception of the esophageal Doppler device) is intermittent and will be available only as long as the operator manually maintains the precise position of the probe head in the optimal sonic window.

In a personal experience with a Doppler device using all three sonic windows in a group of critically ill cardiomyopathy patients with left ventricular ejection fractions (LVEF) of 15% or less, a fellow researcher and I found that our device was unable to calculate believable cardiac outputs. The results varied in an unpredictable way. We were able to obtain adequate Doppler signals in only 40% of our patient sample and were unable to determine on which patients the device would give us accurate results. Age, sex, race, height, weight, and operator did not predict success in obtaining cardiac output measures with our particular Doppler device.

Contrary to our experience, published studies indicate an acceptable correlation between measures of cardiac output obtained by Doppler and thermodilution techniques.[5] Some users report problems keeping the probe head consistently positioned at the precise angle needed for maximal signal from the ascending aorta. The smallest movements of the operator's hand or wrist result in a drastic reduction in the reported cardiac output. Additionally, patients complain of discomfort from the probe head placement, particularly when the patient's anatomy requires inward moderate pressure in order to achieve an adequate signal.

Despite the reported high correlation of the Doppler method of measuring cardiac output with Fick and thermodilution techniques, day-to-day use illustrates that this technology is time and personnel intensive. Difficulties in determining actual aortic diameter and a variety of other methodologic issues need to be resolved before the Doppler devices will be considered a preferred, valid, and reliable replacement for present invasive procedures.

## TRANSTHORACIC ELECTRICAL BIOIMPEDANCE

Transthoracic electrical bioimpedance (TEB) is another noninvasive technique to obtain estimates of cardiac output. The technique is also known as skin impedance, plethysmography, thoracic electrical impedance (TEI), and impedance cardiography. This technique calculates cardiac outputs based on the change in the resistance of the subject's skin to a low voltage current over time. This resistance is greatly influenced by blood flow, because blood is an excellent conductor of electricity. As the blood surges forward into the systemic and thoracic circulations during ventricular systole, there is a decrease in the impedance to the introduced current.

This rather interesting approach to noninvasively measure stroke volume and cardiac output was initially proposed by

Nyoboer in 1959[6] and again in 1966 by Kubicek and co-workers.[7] Bioimpedance was first shown to have clinical use to measure cardiac output while evaluating cardiovascular performance of astronauts.[7] Both studies used such factors as resistivity of blood, the distance between sensing electrodes, base impedance level, and the pulsatile impedance changes to calculate stroke volume based on the thoracic electrical impedance. The formula of Kubicek and co-workers varied from that of Nyoboer's in that it calculated the variation of impedance due to cardiac function in an indirect manner. Kubicek and co-workers proposed the concept that the rate of blood flow during ventricular systole is constant throughout the cardiac cycle. It also assumed that the thorax and the aorta could be thought of as parallel cylinders of equivalent length. Until recently, Kubicek's equation was the primary impedance method used for the determination of cardiac outputs because it was believed to be less affected by ventilatory changes. The electrode placement of Kubicek and co-workers was often thought to have acceptable correlations with invasive techniques of cardiac output measurements.

The formula and technique of the work of Kubicek and co-workers have drawbacks. The four electrodes used to introduce and to sense electrical current are applied using straps or bands that encircle the chest at the horizontal level of the xiphoid process and the base of the neck. These bands are uncomfortable to the subject and may restrict respiratory movements of the chest wall. Other drawbacks include the need to determine the resistance of each subject's blood and the distance between the inner set of electrodes. This latter measurement was of particular concern, since individual anatomical variance, sex, and weight could cause considerable differences in this subjective appraisal. Studies failed to produce cardiac output results with a high correlation to thermodilution techniques.[8]

The work of Sramek[9] and later Bernstein[10] modified the equation of Kubicek and co-workers by removing the need for determining blood resistance and measuring the distance between the inner set of electrodes in their calculations. They conceptualized the thorax as a truncated cone and formulated a constant based on the patient's height corrected for idealized body weight for inclusion into their equation. This new formula concerns itself with the actual volume of thoracic tissue in the electrically active area under study.

Based on the Sramek-Bernstein equation, the Noninvasive Continuous Cardiac Output Monitor (NCCOM) was developed. To promote patient comfort, the device uses eight to ten disposable ECG electrodes instead of the Kubicek band technique. These electrodes are placed on the subject's body in the following configuration: two on each side of the neck, as close as possible to the clavicles at the neck base; and two sets of electrodes (two individual ECG electrodes on each side) placed vertically at the intersection of the midaxillary line and the lateral aspect of the xiphoid process (Figure 6-1). The ninth and tenth electrodes, although recommended for an optimal ECG signal, are optional and are placed on the chest in a configuration that gives the operator the best ECG signal possible (often a standard lead II). The only things the operator must do to use the device are to attach the electrodes to the patient, enter the "L" value (thoracic length based on height, weight, and sex—obtained from a convenient chart located on top of the machine), and turn on the apparatus. While operating, the NCCOM3 can display six different variables:

1. Thoracic fluid index
2. Ventricular ejection time
3. Ejection velocity index
4. Stroke volume
5. Heart rate
6. Cardiac output

These variables can be updated to show new values after every 12 accepted beats, can be averaged over a 10-second period, or can be displayed in response to every accepted beat.

In the NCCOM3 device a very low voltage current (1 mV) is applied to the thorax. Changes in the volume and velocity of blood flow through the thoracic aorta cause an alteration in thoracic conductivity of the current. These changes over time have been shown to be proportional to the stroke volume, and therefore when the heart rate is known an estimate of the cardiac output can be obtained since cardiac output = stroke volume × heart rate. The NCCOM3 must have clean ECG and bioimpedance signals in order to give valid estimates of cardiac output.

With the use of the NCCOM3 device and this new electrode array, two studies demonstrated high correlations between cardiac output measures obtained by the TEB method and thermodilution

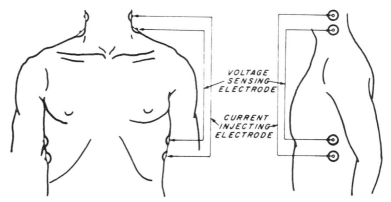

**Figure 6-1** Placement of electrodes for transthoracic electrical bioimpedance determination of cardiac output. *Source:* Reprinted from "Continuous Noninvasive Real-Time Monitoring of Stroke Volume and Cardiac Output by Thoracic Electrical Bioimpedance" by DP Bernstein in *Critical Care Medicine* (1986;14[10]:898–901), Copyright © 1986, Williams & Wilkins Company.

---

technique ($r = 0.88, 0.83$).[11,12] Both studies examined small samples ($n = 17, 16$) of "critically" or "desperately" ill patients for large numbers of simultaneous TEB and thermodilution measurements. Intubation and ventilatory support of their subjects did not appear to affect the results. Conditions under which the TEB has difficulty include

- presence of metal in the chest or chest wall
- sepsis
- hypertension
- oily skin
- dysrhythmias, tachycardia of greater than 150 beats per minute
- aortic valvular insufficiency
- ventricular septal defects
- the use of electrocautery.

Inadequate skin preparation for the electrodes may be another source of variation. Bernstein also noted that the TEB device tended to show its greatest difference from the thermodilution technique in situations in which the thermodilution was very low

(< 2 liters/min). In these patients, the TEB could overestimate the cardiac output by as much as 50% to 100%. The manufacturer does not recommend the use of the NCCOM3 on patients with functioning pacemakers.

One of the advantages to the use of the TEB devices is the ability to display a continuous stream of cardiovascular data, including cardiac output, with no operator intervention after its initial setup. To receive the cardiac output data constantly, the electrode patches must remain on the subject during the entire time period of data collection. For many patients, the presence of such a large number of electrodes just for impedance data, in addition to five electrodes for ECG monitoring in the intensive care unit, became problematic due to electrode patch–induced skin irritation, impairment of neck movements, and the "spaghetti factor." With the presence of 13 to 15 electrodes on the body as well as their connecting electrode leads, the simple rearrangement of blankets by the patient can turn into a confusing and frustrating maze of twisted wires, restricting movement. Despite these drawbacks, it should be remembered that the discomforts may be more tolerable than those experienced by persons with a thermodilution catheter in place for cardiovascular monitoring.

## SUMMARY

Despite the technical and/or reliability problems encountered with the Doppler and bioimpedance methods of measuring cardiac output, these two techniques have potential for future use and development. Both require further refinement in their technical application. There is a need for further study in a wider variety of clinical and patient settings. Other methods for noninvasive cardiac outputs are also being tested and hold additional promise for the eventual development of an ideal cardiac output technique.[13]

---

REFERENCES

1. Wetzel RC, Latson TW: Major errors in thermodilution cardiac output measurement during rapid volume infusion. *Anesthesiology* 1985;62:684–689.

2. Levett JM, Replogle RL: Thermodilution cardiac output: A critical analysis and review of literature. *J Surg Res* 1979;27:392–404.

3. Ihlen H, Amlie J, Dale J, Forfang K, Nitter-Hange S, Otterstad J, Simonsen S, Myhre E: Determination of cardiac output by Doppler echocardiography. *Br Heart J* 1984;51:54–59.

4. Christie J, Sheldahl LM, Tristani FE, Sagar KB, Ptacin MJ, Wann S: Determination of stroke volume and cardiac output during exercise: Comparison of stroke volume and cardiac output during exercise: Comparison of two-dimensional and Doppler echocardiography, Fick oximetry, and thermodilution. *Circulation* 1987;76:539–547.

5. Sabbah HN, Khaja F, Brymer JF, McFarland TM, Albert DE, Snyder JE, Goldstein S, Stein PD: Noninvasive evaluation of left ventricular performance based on peak aortic blood acceleration measured with a continuous-wave Doppler velocity meter. *Circulation* 1986;74:323–329.

6. Nyoboer J: *Impedance Plethysmography.* Springfield, IL, Charles C Thomas, 1959.

7. Kubicek WG, Karnegis JN, Patterson RP, et al: Development and evaluation of an impedance cardiac output system. *Aerospace Med* 1966;37:1208–1215.

8. Donovan KD, Dobb GJ, Woods WPD, Hockings BE: Comparison of transthoracic electrical impedance and thermodilution methods for measuring cardiac output. *Crit Care Med* 1986;14:1038–1044.

9. Sramek B: Noninvasive technique for measurement of cardiac output by means of electrical impedance, in *Proceedings of the Fifth International Conference on Electrical Bioimpedance.* Tokyo, 1981.

10. Bernstein DP: A new stroke volume equation for thoracic electrical bioimpedance: Theory and rationale. *Crit Care Med* 1986;14:904–909.

11. Bernstein DP: Continuous noninvasive real-time monitoring of stroke volume and cardiac output by thoracic electrical bioimpedance. *Crit Care Med* 1986;14:898–901.

12. Appel P, Kram HB, Mackabee J, Fleming AW, Shoemaker WC: Comparison of measurements of cardiac output by bioimpedance and thermodilution in severely ill surgical patients. *Crit Care Med* 1986;14:933–935.

13. Tremper KK, Hufstedler SM, Barker SJ, Zaccari J, Harris D, Anderson S, Roohk V: Continuous noninvasive estimation of cardiac output by electrical bioimpedance: An experimental study in dogs. *Crit Care Med* 1986;14:231–233.

---

**RECOMMENDED READING**

Barash PG (ed): *Continuous Cardiac Output Monitoring with ACCUCOM: A Progress Report.* Princeton Junction, NJ, Communications Media for Education, 1987.

Bolely T, Curtis JJ, Walls JT, Reid JC: Noninvasive cardiac output determination: A comparison with thermodilution. *Heart Lung* 1987;16:289.

Grasberger RC, Yeston NS: Less-invasive cardiac output monitoring by earpiece densitometry. *Crit Care Med* 1986;14:577–579.

Kubicek WG, Patterson RP, Witsoe DA: Impedance cardiography as a noninvasive method of monitoring cardiac function and other parameters of the cardiovascular system. *Ann NY Acad Sci* 1970;170:724–732.

Lamberts R, Visser KR, Zijlstra WG: *Impedance Cardiography*. Amsterdam, Van Gorcum, 1984.

McLennan FM, Haites NE, MacKenzie JD, Daniel MK, Rawles JM: Reproducibility of linear cardiac output measurement by Doppler ultrasound alone. *Br Heart J* 1986;55:25–31.

Mohapatra SN: *Noninvasive Cardiovascular Monitoring by Electrical Impedance Technique*. London, Pitman Medical, 1981.

Nishimura RA, Callahan MJ, Schaff HV, Ilstrup DM, Miller FA, Tajik AJ: Noninvasive measurement of cardiac output by continuous-wave Doppler echocardiography: Initial experience and review of the literature. *Mayo Clin Proc* 1984;59:484–489.

Spinale FG, Reines HD, Crawford FA: Comparison of bioimpedance and thermodilution methods for determining cardiac output: Experimental and clinical studies, in *Proceedings of the 1987 Annual Meeting of the Southern Thoracic Surgical Association*, 1987.

Trempter KK: Continuous noninvasive cardiac output: Are we getting there? *Crit Care Med* 1987;15:278–279.

Ultrasound cardiac output units. *Health Devices* 1988;17(6–7):195–211.

# CHAPTER 7

# Continuous
# ST-Segment Analysis

*John M. Clochesy*

# 7

Significant myocardial ischemia can occur in the absence of chest pain. Continuous ST-segment monitoring shows that painless ST-segment changes occur about twice as often as those associated with pain.[1] Simultaneous positron emission tomography (PET) and ST-segment analysis showed evidence of ischemia in all cases of painless ST-segment depression and in 97% of the cases of ST-segment depression with angina.[2] Use of continuous ST-segment monitoring began in exercise electrocardiography of patients with angina and later found use in 24-hour recordings of ambulatory patients suspected of coronary artery spasm.[3] The frequency response of monitors used for ST-segment analysis has been a concern.[4]

## SIGNIFICANCE

Biagini and associates performed continuous ECG recordings in ten patients in a coronary care unit.[5] During the study period, the nursing staff detected 31 transient ischemic attacks, 9 of which were asymptomatic. Analysis of the concurrent ECG recordings revealed 213 ischemic episodes. The tapes were played back in real time on the coronary care unit central station monitor. A cardiologist, who had the option of stopping the tapes and replaying them, recognized only 48% of the episodes when the tracing in question was randomly mixed with three others on the monitor. When only one ECG tracing was on the monitor, the cardiologist was able to detect 92% of the episodes. It is a credit to the nurses that they detected 14% of the episodes when a cardiologist with no duties other than monitor observation detected only 48%. Since it is impossible to assign one observer per patient per monitor to observe the majority of ST-segment changes in coronary care unit patients, a computerized monitoring system is indicated.

In a study of patients with severe angina awaiting coronary bypass grafting and patients 3 years after myocardial infarction, Angelhed and associates found that ST-segment analysis was sensitive (92%–94%) in the angina group and less sensitive (50%) in the postinfarct group in identifying critical coronary lesions. Specificity for both groups was 68% to 76%.[6]

## APPLICATION

Microcomputer-assisted multichannel ECG monitoring systems compute ST-segment depression/elevation and ST-segment slope. Kotrly and associates modified a Marquette Electronics MAC (microcomputer augmented cardiograph) and connected it to a four-channel Hewlett-Packard nonfade oscilloscope for intraoperative ST-segment monitoring.[7] Such monitoring is now available as part of Marquette Electronics Series 7000 bedside monitoring system. Other vendors are developing similar microcomputer-based systems. Although highly accurate, these systems do falsely detect some changes due to artifact as ST-segment changes.[8] The incidence of perioperative myocardial ischemia for patients with known ischemic heart disease undergoing noncardiac surgery ranges from 20% to 38%.[9,10] ST-segment analysis may be indicated for all such patients.

ST-segment monitoring may be especially helpful in patients receiving thrombolytic therapy or following percutaneous transluminal coronary angioplasty (PTCA). During thrombolytic therapy, ST-segment monitoring identified successful reperfusion with 89% sensitivity and 82% specificity.[11] In a study of 16 patients following PTCA, five spontaneous, asymptomatic episodes of ST-segment deviation were detected in two patients.[12] Such monitoring may help in determining the efficacy of PTCA and may detect patients in need of further therapy prior to the onset of angina or infarction.

### REFERENCES

1. Balasubramanian V, Lahiri A, Green HL, Stott FD, Raftery EB: Ambulatory ST-segment monitoring: Problems, pitfalls, solutions, and clinical application. *Br Heart J* 1980;44:419–425.

2. Deanfield JE, Shea M, Ribiero P, de Landsheere CM, Wilson RA, Horlock P, Selwyn AP: Transient ST-segment depression as a marker of myocardial ischemia during daily life. *Am J Cardiol* 1984;54:1195–1200.

3. Biagini A, Mazzei MG, Carpeggiani C, Testa R, Antonelli R, Michelassi C, L'Abbate A, Maseri A: Vasospastic ischemic mechanism of frequent asymptomatic transient ST-T changes during continuous electrocardiographic monitoring in selected unstable angina patients. *Am Heart J* 1982;103:13–19.

4. Bragg-Resmschel DA, Anderson CM, Winkle RA: Frequency response characteristics of ambulatory ECG monitoring systems and their implications for ST-segment analysis. *Am Heart J* 1982;103:20–31.

5. Biagini A, L'Abbate A, Testa R, Carpeggiani C, Mazzei MG, Michelassi C, Benassi A, Riva A, Marchesi C, Maseri A: Unreliability of conventional visual electrocardiographic monitoring for detection of transient ST-segment changes in a coronary care unit. *Eur Heart J* 1984;5:784–791.

6. Angelhed JE, Bjuro TI, Ejdeback J, Selin K, Schlossman D, Griffith LSC, Bergstrand R, Vedin A, Wilhelmsson C: Computer-aided exercise electrocardiographic testing and coronary arteriography in patients with angina pectoris and with myocardial infarction. *Br Heart J* 1984;52:140–146.

7. Kotrly KJ, Kotter GS, Mortara D, Kampine JP: Intraoperative detection of myocardial ischemia with an ST-segment trend monitoring system. *Anesth Analg* 1984;63:343–345.

8. Oyama T, Ishihara H, Tanioka F, Matsuki A, Aida N, Ishii H: Clinical application of arrhythmia analyzer in ICU. *Int J Clin Monit Comput* 1987;4(2):99–104.

9. Griffin RM, Kaplan JA: Myocardial ischaemia during noncardiac surgery: A comparison of different lead systems using computerized ST-segment analysis. *Anesthesia* 1987;42:155–159.

10. Roy WL, Edelist G, Gilbert B: Myocardial ischemia during noncardiac surgical procedures in patients with coronary artery disease. *Anesthesiology* 1979;51:393–397.

11. Krucoff MW, Green CE, Satler LF, Miller FC, Pallas RS, Kent KM, del Negro AA, Pearle DL, Fletcher RD, Rackley CE: Noninvasive detection of coronary artery patency using continuous ST-segment monitoring. *Am J Cardiol* 1986;57:916–922.

12. Hoberg E, Schwarz F, Voggenreiter U, Kuebler W: Holter monitoring before, during, and after percutaneous transluminal coronary angioplasty for evaluation of high-resolution trend recordings of leads $CM_5$, and $CC_5$ for ST-segment analysis. *Am J Cardiol* 1987;60:796–800.

**RECOMMENDED READING**

Savage MP, Squires LS, Hopkins JT, Raichlen JS, Park CH, Chung EK: Usefulness of ST-segment depression as a sign of coronary artery disease when confined to the postexercise recovery period. *Am J Cardiol* 1987;60:1405–1406.

# External Pacemakers

*John M. Clochesy*

# 8

## HISTORY OF EXTERNAL PACEMAKERS

The first successful external pacing was reported by Zoll in 1952.[1] Two millisecond pulses were given using a hypodermic needle placed into the subcutaneous tissues of the chest wall with a skin ground electrode. This procedure had several drawbacks, including painful skeletal muscle stimulation due to high pacing currents. Interest in external pacing dwindled with the introduction of transvenous pacing.[2]

Interest in external pacing renewed with ZMI Corporation's introduction of the Zoll NTP (noninvasive temporary pacemaker) in the fall of 1984. Since that time, noninvasive pacing has been recognized by the American Heart Association as helpful in patients whose primary problem is impulse formation or conduction and who have preserved myocardial function.[3] Its use is included in the treatment algorithm for bradycardia.[4]

## PACEMAKER CHARACTERISTICS

Like other cardiac pacemakers, pulse rate and output (stimulus strength) can be set (Figure 8-1). The output range is significantly greater than the 0 to 20 mA range of the regular temporary pulse generator or the 0 to 28 mA range of the high-output pulse generator. Additionally, the external noninvasive temporary pacemaker (NTP) has an ECG monitor and strip chart recorder.

91

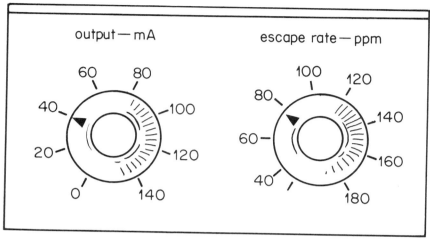

**Figure 8-1**   Controls of external pacemaker.

## Pacing Threshold

Falk and associates reported thresholds for external pacing in a study of 16 volunteers and 15 cardiology patients. The results of this study are summarized in Table 8-1. It was not possible to pace one patient with severe cardiomyopathy; this patient had a very high stimulation threshold for transvenous pacing. The mean pacing threshold for patients with hemodynamically unstable bradycardia was higher (78 mA) than the mean threshold for patients who were hemodynamically stable (51 mA).[5] Worley and Bride found mean thresholds of 67 mA and 73 mA in two groups of patients with acute myocardial infarction. The thresholds ranged from 48 to 100 mA.[6]

## Pulse Duration and Strength

Pulse generators used for temporary transvenous and epicardial pacing deliver pulses of 1.8 msec in duration. When short-duration pulses are used for external pacing, painful skin sensation and muscle twitching occur. A variety of pulse durations from 1 to 50 msec have been studied. Zoll recommends a 40-msec pulse.[7]

**Table 8-1**   Pacing Thresholds Using an External Noninvasive Temporary
Pacemaker

| Subjects | Number | Threshold |
|---|---|---|
| Volunteer medical students, house staff, and attending staff who were free of heart disease | 16 | Mean = 54 mA<br>Range = 42–60 mA |
| Cardiology patients with need for temporary pacemaker | 15 | Mean = 56 mA<br>Range = 42–80 mA |

*Source:* Adapted with permission from *New England Journal of Medicine* (1983;309:1166–1168), Copyright ©1983, Massachusetts Medical Society.

Geddes and associates suggest that for minimal pain, the optimal stimulus duration is about 10 msec.[8]

## Electrode Size and Placement

Large electrodes 5 to 10 cm in diameter are used to decrease transcutaneous resistance and pain due to skeletal muscle stimulation.[5,9,10] The negative electrode is placed on the left anterior chest wall near the apex (standard lead $V_5$).[10,11] The size and proper placement of the external pacing electrodes are shown in Figure 8-2.

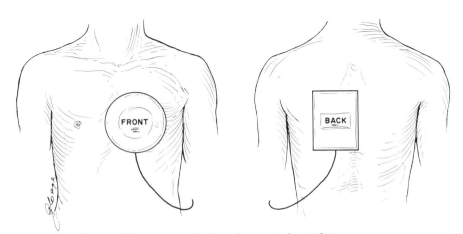

**Figure 8-2** Size and placement of external pacing electrodes.

## Pacing Modes

The Zoll NTP operates in the demand (VVI) mode. By disconnecting the built-in ECG monitor the device will operate in the asynchronous (VOO) mode.[5,6,12]

## EFFECTIVENESS OF EXTERNAL PACING

Falk and associates studied the effectiveness of external pacing in healthy volunteers and in patients with acute myocardial infarction, severe toxicity due to digoxin, and nonsustained ventricular tachycardia.[5] Zoll and Zoll studied 134 patients in five centers. The external pacemaker produced an electrical response in 78.4% of the patients, including 43 patients in cardiac arrest.[9] Sixteen patients had electrical activity restored but had electromechanical dissociation (EMD).

## MYOCARDIAL INJURY

A single animal study has evaluated the damage that may be caused by the transcutaneous electrical stimulation of the heart.[13] Ten dogs received 100-mA 20-msec duration pulses at a rate of 80 stimuli per minute for 30 minutes. Seventy-two hours later the animals were sacrificed and the heart, lungs, and tissues of the chest wall were examined. There were gross and microscopic lesions in both the right and left ventricles consistent with electrically induced myocardial damage in all of the hearts. The lesions were not extensive and would not be expected to cause clinically detectable changes in cardiovascular status. Short-term use of an external pacemaker does not appear to produce significant myocardial damage.

## IMPLEMENTING EXTERNAL PACING

The main advantage of external pacing is that the adhesive patch electrodes can be promptly applied by personnel with little specialized training or experience. If the patient is hemodynamically stable, the skin is cleansed to remove electrode paste, soap, powder, lotion, and dead skin. If hair will prevent good contact, the hair can be clipped with scissors. Shaving should not be done because it may produce small nicks in the skin, lowering impedance to current flow and resulting in severe pain during pacing.[12]

The rectangular "back" electrode is applied first. The electrode is placed between the scapula and the spine at the level of the heart. Next, the round "front" electrode is applied to the anterior left chest near the apex. After the electrodes are positioned, the pacing threshold is determined. The pacing artifact is longer in duration than those seen with transvenous pacemakers. The artifact will be 40 msec, or one small box on the ECG strip. Once the threshold is determined, the output is adjusted to a level slightly higher. The pacing threshold should decrease slightly since the transthoracic impedance decreases with repeated stimuli.

The effectiveness of the external pacemaker is then evaluated by documenting the following:

- cardiac rhythm, blood pressure, and level of consciousness prior to pacing

- threshold

- cardiac rhythm, blood pressure, and level of consciousness during pacing

- any skeletal muscle response or pain due to pacing[14]

Once successful pacing has been established, the patient can be prepared for transvenous pacemaker insertion. If the patient is not a candidate for a transvenous pacemaker, pacing is periodically interrupted to assess and document underlying cardiac rhythm and blood pressure. The Zoll NTP is shown in Figure 8-3.

Limitations of external pacing include situations in which the stimulation threshold exceeds patient comfort or the current range of the pulse generator. These situations include dilated cardiomyopathy, high cardiac stimulation thresholds, obesity, hyperinflated lung disease, large pleural or pericardial effusions, poor electrode contact with the skin, and hypoxemia.

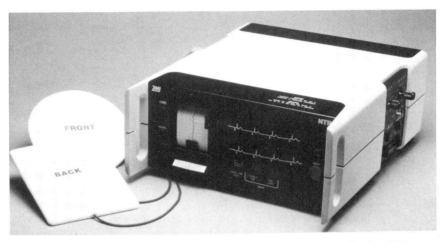

**Figure 8-3** Zoll NTP. *Source:* Courtesy of ZMI Corporation, Cambridge, MA.

**REFERENCES**

1. Zoll PM: Resuscitation of the heart in ventricular standstill by external electrical stimulation. *N Engl J Med* 1952;248:768–771.

2. Furman S, Robinson G: Use of an intracardiac pacemaker in the correction of total heart block. *Surg Forum* 1958;9:245–248.

3. Thevenet A, Hodges PC, Lillehei CW: The use of myocardial electrode inserted percutaneously for control of complete atrioventricular block by artificial pacemaker. *Dis Chest* 1958;34:621–631.

4. American Heart Association: Standards and guidelines for cardiopulmonary resuscitation (CPR) and emergency cardiac care (ECC). *JAMA* 1986;255:2905–2984.

5. Falk RH, Zoll PM, Zoll RH: Safety and efficacy of noninvasive cardiac pacing: A preliminary report. *N Engl J Med* 1983;309:1166–1168.

6. Worley SJ, Bride WM: External transthoracic pacing in patients with acute myocardial infarction, in Califf RM, Wagner GS (eds): *Acute Coronary Care 1987*. Boston, Martinus Nijhoff Publishing, 1987.

7. Zoll PM, Zoll RH, Belgard AH: External noninvasive electric stimulation of the heart. *Crit Care Med* 1981;9:393–394.

8. Geddes LA, Babbs CF, Voorhees WD, Foster KS, Aronson AL: Choice of the optimum pulse duration for precordial cardiac pacing: A theoretical study. *PACE* 1985;8:862–869.

9. Zoll PM, Zoll RH: Noninvasive temporary cardiac stimulation. *Crit Care Med* 1985;13:925–926.

10. Geddes LA, Voorhees WD, Babbs CF, Sisken R, DeFord J: Precordial pacing windows. *PACE* 1984;719:806–812.

11. Falk RH, Ngai STA: External cardiac pacing: Influence of electrode placement on pacing threshold. *Crit Care Med* 1986;14:931–932.

12. Mickus D, Mohnahan KJ, Brown C: Exciting external pacemakers. *Am J Nurs* 1986;86:403–405.

13. Kicklighter EJ, Syverud SA, Dalsey WC, Hedges JR, Van der Bel-Kahn JA: Pathological aspects of transcutaneous cardiac pacing. *Am J Emerg Med* 1985;3:108–113.

14. Persons CB: Transcutaneous pacing: Meeting the challenge. *Focus Crit Care* 1987;14(1):13–19.

---

**RECOMMENDED READING**

Dalsey WC, Syverud SA, Troot A: Transcutaneous cardiac pacing. *J Emerg Med* 1984;1:201–205.

Feldman MD, Zoll PM, Aroesty JM, Gervino EV, Pasternak RC, McKay RG: Hemodynamic responses to noninvasive external cardiac pacing. *Am J Med* 1988;84:395–400.

Transcutaneous pacemakers. *Health Devices* 1988;February:39–46.

# Automatic Implantable Cardioverter-Defibrillator

*Carol M. Mravinac*

# 9

Recurrent ventricular dysrhythmias and sudden death are often difficult to treat. When conventional or investigational antidysrhythmic drug therapy is ineffective, an automatic implantable cardioverter-defibrillator (AICD) may be used. The AICD was developed by Mirowski and associates and was first tested in humans in 1980. The device continuously monitors the patient's heart rate and rhythm.[1] Current models are able to identify and treat both ventricular fibrillation and ventricular tachycardia by releasing a small amount of electrical current internally to the patient.

## THE AICD SYSTEM

The AICD consists of two main components: the pulse generator and the electrodes. The pulse generator has the capacity to sense changes in heart rate and QRS complex morphology. Lithium batteries allow the defibrillator to deliver 100 shocks or monitor the patient's cardiac rhythm for 3 years.[2] The size of the generator is $11.2 \times 7.11 \times 2.54$ cm, and it weighs 290 grams. The outer shell is made of titanium.[3]

Several types of electrodes are used with the sensing component of the pulse generator. The various AICD leads are shown in Figure 9-1. Usually a bipolar endocardial lead or two unipolar sutureless myocardial leads detect changes in heart rate. Two ventricular patch electrodes or a superior vena caval spring wire lead and a ventricular patch electrode sense changes in morphology and deliver the defibrillation/cardioversion pulse. In Figure 9-2 two unipolar sutureless myocardial sensing leads and two ventricular patch leads are shown in place.

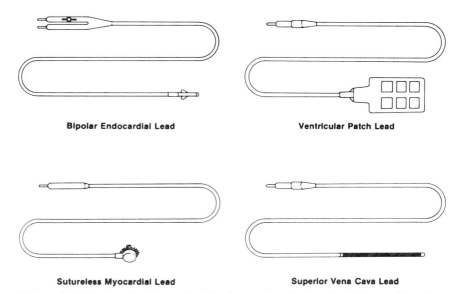

**Bipolar Endocardial Lead**

**Ventricular Patch Lead**

**Sutureless Myocardial Lead**

**Superior Vena Cava Lead**

**Figure 9-1** Various leads used with the automatic implantable cardioverter-defibrillator. *Source:* Reprinted from *AICD Physicians Manual* (p 2) with permission of Cardiac Pacemakers Inc, Copyright © 1985.

The AICD unit is tested prior to implantation and is programmed with the individual patient's defibrillation threshold. The AICD senses ventricular tachycardia or ventricular fibrillation within 5 to 20 seconds. An additional 5 to 15 seconds are required to charge the pulse generator before the first of a possible four countershocks is delivered. The first pulse, or countershock, is usually 23 to 28 joules. If the first pulse is ineffective in terminating the lethal rhythm, additional pulses, up to a total of four, are released. The second through fourth pulses have an increased energy output of 28 to 37 joules. These additional pulses are delivered in a 35-second period. A 35-second period to reset the AICD to normal monitoring operation follows the fourth pulse.[3] These events are schematically represented in Figure 9-3.

## DIFFERENT AICD MODELS

Two AICD models are available: the AICD-B and the AICD-BR. The AICD-B pulse generator senses both changes in rate and

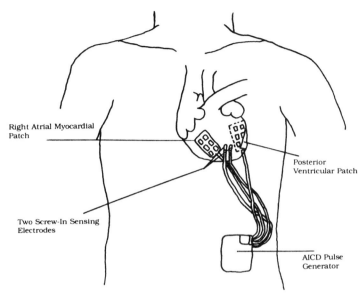

**Figure 9-2** Placement of unipolar sensing and ventricular patch electrodes for the AICD. *Source:* Reprinted with permission from *Focus on Critical Care Nursing* (1986;13[6]:55), Copyright © 1986, The CV Mosby Company.

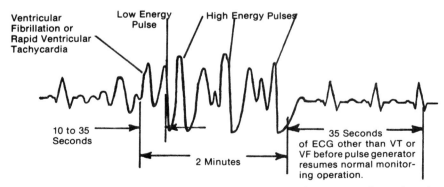

**Figure 9-3** Dysrhythmia detection, pulse delivery, and resetting of sensing circuitry in the AICD, VT, ventricular tachycardia; VF, ventricular fibrillation. *Source:* Reprinted from *AICD Physicians Manual* (p 3) with permission of Cardiac Pacemakers Inc, Copyright © 1985.

changes in morphology. It is less likely to deliver an energy pulse for changes in a patient's rate, for example in a patient with supraventricular tachycardia. Although it will deliver fewer unwarranted shocks, it requires a longer period of time to detect ventricular dysrhythmias. The longer detection time may lead to periods of hypotension during ventricular tachycardia.

The AICD-BR pulse generator senses increases in rate only and may monitor a wider range of ventricular dysrhythmias. Since the unit does not sense changes in the morphology of the QRS complex, it may deliver unnecessary shocks during supraventricular dysrhythmias, such as atrial fibrillation, atrial flutter, and supraventricular tachycardia. This model is usually used in conjunction with antidysrhythmics to control the patient's ventricular response to atrial dysrhythmias.

## INDICATIONS

Initial clinical studies of the AICD were conducted at the Johns Hopkins Hospital between February 1980 and March 1981. Subjects included patients with known coronary artery disease who had survived at least two prehospital cardiac arrests with documentation of ventricular fibrillation.[2] Since these initial trials, the device has received approval of the Food and Drug Administration and patient selection criteria were broadened to include patients who are at risk for recurrence of sudden death, have a documented history of ventricular tachycardia, and are with or without known cardiac disease.

### Sudden Cardiac Death

Ventricular irritability with or without chest pain that occurs outside the hospital and results in abrupt electrical instability is commonly referred to as sudden cardiac death.[4] Ventricular fibrillation precipitated by ventricular tachycardia is the dysrhythmia most commonly associated with sudden cardiac death. Studies suggest that the majority of sudden cardiac death survivors have no evidence of myocardial ischemia or infarction.[5] As many as 47% of survivors of sudden cardiac death have a recurrence within 2 years of the initial episode.[6]

## Electrophysiologic Mechanism

Disturbances in cardiac impulse conduction that result in ventricular dysrhythmias are primarily due to reentry.[7] Depolarization and repolarization usually occur uniformly. However, when an impulse is slowed or blocked, it may take an alternate pathway. The differences in impulse velocity and conduction on retrograde pathways may result in ventricular dysrhythmias.[8] Prompt application of an electrical discharge to the fibrillating heart results in termination of the dysrhythmia. Prior to the development of the AICD, application of high-energy dose transthoracic impulses was the most successful method of defibrillation in patients with recurrent sudden cardiac death.

Mirowski and associates developed the miniaturized, low-voltage defibrillator using two concepts:

1. Low energy levels could be used to successfully terminate ventricular fibrillation.
2. Probability density function could be used to sense ventricular fibrillation.

Their studies demonstrated that low voltage defibrillation was possible. Additionally, the energy could be delivered to the myocardium by an intracardiac catheter.[2] This supports the idea that only a critical mass, or small area of the myocardium, is needed to successfully defibrillate.[9]

The sensing mechanism of the AICD is based on the probability density function of ventricular activity.[2] The device identifies the electrocardiogram and statistically analyzes the changes in amplitude of each waveform (cardiac cycle). The sensing circuit measures the average time the ECG spends at the isoelectric line. During ventricular tachycardia and ventricular fibrillation there are few signals on the isoelectric line.[9] The unit recognizes this change in electrical activity and a defibrillating impulse (shock) is delivered to the patient (Figure 9-4).

Electrophysiological studies help to differentiate between electrical events originating in the ventricles and those originating elsewhere. Supraventricular tachycardia may have a morphology similar to certain forms of ventricular tachycardia. Patients who experience sustained ventricular tachycardia are studied in the electrophysiology laboratory prior to antidysrhythmic or surgical

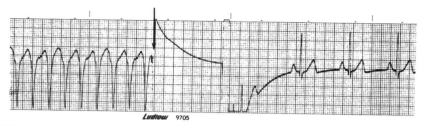

**Figure 9-4** Recognition and defibrillation of ventricular tachycardia by an AICD. *Source:* Reprinted with permission from *Focus on Critical Care Nursing* (1986;13[6]:56), Copyright ©1986, The CV Mosby Company.

therapy using programmed electrical stimulation.[7] The dysrhythmia is induced in a controlled setting. Various antidysrhythmic agents, pacing techniques, and defibrillation are used to terminate the induced dysrhythmia. For patients who have survived an episode of sudden cardiac death and in whom the dysrhythmia cannot be induced during electrophysiological study, implantation of the AICD is considered.[10]

## CONTRAINDICATIONS

Patients who fear dependency on a device or who worry about its reliability may not be considered for AICD implantation. Early data show that patients with severely compromised left ventricular function do not benefit from this type of device. These patients have a 1-year mortality rate about ten times that of comparable patients without the AICD.[10]

## METHODS OF IMPLANTATION

Five surgical approaches are used for implanting the AICD unit. The choice of approach depends on

- the size of the patient's heart
- any prior chest surgery
- the extensiveness of the operative procedure
- the condition of the patient.[3,10]

The lead systems serve several purposes. They are to sense changes in heart rate and morphology and to deliver a defibrillating/cardioverting energy pulse. Changes in heart rate can be detected by either a bipolar endocardial lead inserted intravascularly and positioned in the right ventricular apex or with two unipolar sutureless myocardial leads attached to the left ventricular wall. Two ventricular patch electrodes are frequently lysed to sense morphologic changes occurring with ventricular fibrillation and ventricular tachycardia. These ventricular patch electrodes can be placed using one of four approaches. The most common surgical approach is a median sternotomy, since this procedure often accompanies other antidysrhythmic or revascularization procedures. If the patient previously had aortocoronary bypass surgery, a left thoracotomy may be done in an effort to avoid causing additional scar tissue.[11] Although exposure may be limited, a subcostal or subxiphoid incision may be used in patients who do not require other cardiac procedures.[3]

A pocket is made in the left upper quadrant of the abdomen to accommodate the pulse generator.[11] The lead systems are tunneled subcutaneously and connected to it. The complete unit consists of two sensing/defibrillating patch electrodes and two rate-sensing electrodes. Screw-in unipolar myocardial leads or a single endocardial bipolar electrode may be used to monitor heart rate.

## PREOPERATIVE PREPARATION

Three factors are necessary for successful outcome[10]:

1. An adequately prepared patient and family
2. Health care providers who are skilled and experienced in treating patients with malignant dysrhythmias
3. State-of-the-art equipment that is regularly checked for optimal functioning.

Preparing the patient and family for AICD implantation involves a thorough cardiovascular assessment, preoperative education, and psychosocial support. Baseline hemodynamic data and dysrhythmia history are obtained, including specific patterns of ventricular tachycardia and the results of electrophysiological studies. The patient's overall cardiovascular status is evaluated by a maximal treadmill stress test.[10] The results of this test provide the physician with information to set rate parameters in the AICD pulse generator.

If the patient has not had prior surgery, a thorough explanation of why the device is necessary and what type of implantation procedure is planned is provided by physician specialists.[12] Additional support services may also be needed to help the patient overcome the fear of surgery or related anxiety.[12] The care of the preoperative patient is summarized in Table 9-1.

## POSTOPERATIVE CARE

Following AICD implantation, the patient has physiological and psychological needs. All health care team members contribute to the plan of care. Critical care nurses ensure continuity of care by implementing a comprehensive series of interventions based on the individual patient's needs. The needs may be divided into those of the acute stage immediately following surgery and long-term needs for follow-up following hospital discharge.

### Acute Phase Care

Many patients undergoing AICD implantation also have aorto-coronary bypass surgery or other antidysrhythmic procedures that necessitate the use of general anesthesia. The primary focus of the critical care nurse during the first 12 hours is to observe the patient, monitor vital signs, and identify problems that may compromise the patient's cardiopulmonary system. The following case study illustrates a patient who has undergone AICD implantation. A comprehensive patient care plan is provided in Table 9-2.

### Case Study

Mrs. B. was a 58-year-old woman admitted to the hospital on December 22 with ventricular dysrhythmias, a suspected acute myocardial infarction, and symptomatic myocardial ischemia. She was referred to this particular hospital after a month-long history of recurrent, hemodynamically unstable ventricular tachycardia.

**Table 9-1** Preoperative Patient Collaborative Care Plan

| Nursing Diagnoses | Expected Outcomes | Interventions |
|---|---|---|
| Knowledge deficit due to unfamiliar technology (AICD) | Patient/family will verbalize an understanding of the need for the AICD and its capabilities. | 1. Assess patient/family's level of understanding of the AICD. 2. Provide AICD patient manual. 3. Physician discusses the need for the device, procedure, and risks. 4. Nurse discusses the preoperative preparation, medications, length of implant surgery, and recovery unit and critical care unit environments. |
| Potential fear or anxiety due to surgical procedure | Patient will verbalize specific fears about surgery. | 1. Assess patient's concern. 2. Provide patient with consistent information. 3. Provide additional support to patient with social services and psychological counseling. |
| Potential for injury due to possible equipment malfunction | Patient will be free from injury during operative procedure. | 1. Maintain the following equipment in the operating suite: <br>• external and internal defibrillating paddles <br>• 2 defibrillators <br>• electrophysiological pacing equipment <br>• AICD testing devices <br>• sensing leads and AICD pulse generators <br>2. Periodically check all equipment according to institution's electrical safety protocol. |

**Table 9-2** Comprehensive Patient Care Plan for Mrs. B.

| Nursing Diagnoses | Expected Outcomes | Interventions |
|---|---|---|
| Potential decreased cardiac output due to bleeding and ventricular dysrhythmias | Mean systemic blood pressure > 60 mm Hg; chest drainage < 50 ml/hr; any ventricular tachycardia converted with AICD | 1. Monitor vital signs every 15 minutes for first 12 hours, then hourly per unit protocol.<br>2. Monitor and record hemodynamic variables per unit protocol.<br>3. Monitor chest drainage every 15 minutes for the first hour, then hourly.<br>4. Monitor peripheral perfusion by urine output, peripheral pulses, and level of consciousness.<br>5. Replace chest tube blood loss with blood products as ordered.<br>6. Keep external defibrillator available for backup use. |
| Potential impaired gas exchange due to atelectasis | Bilaterally clear breath sounds; spontaneous ventilatory rate of 8–14/min; arterial blood gas values at baseline | 1. Assess breath sounds at the beginning of each shift and as necessary.<br>2. Monitor arterial blood gas values.<br>3. Perform chest physiotherapy every 2 to 4 hours.<br>4. Encourage incentive spirometry hourly once extubated.<br>5. Encourage progressive activity and ambulation. |
| Impaired verbal communication due to endotracheal intubation | Able to communicate needs while intubated | 1. Explain all procedures simply.<br>2. Ask questions that require yes or no answers.<br>3. Provide word board or paper and pencil. |

**Table 9-2** *continued*

| Nursing Diagnoses | Expected Outcomes | Interventions |
|---|---|---|
| Impaired skin integrity due to surgical incisions | Wounds remain intact, without drainage or redness. | 1. Monitor temperature every 4 hours.<br>2. Observe and record condition of all incisions every shift.<br>3. Monitor white blood cell count daily.<br>4. Cleanse incisions according to unit protocol. |
| Potential for infection due to surgical incisions and invasive lines | Temperature is normal; white blood cell count is within normal limits. | 1. Monitor temperature every 4 hours.<br>2. Monitor white blood cell count daily.<br>3. Wash hands before and after all patient contact.<br>4. Use aseptic technique for all dressing changes. |
| Alteration in comfort; pain | Pain is relieved. | 1. Assess type, location, and duration of pain.<br>2. Change patient's position frequently.<br>3. Administer analgesics when requested and every 4 hours for 3 days. |
| Sleep deprivation due to ICU environment and routine | Patient will have at least one 4-hour period of sleep beginning on first postoperative day. | 1. Provide quiet environment by lowering lights, restricting visitors, and minimizing noise.<br>2. Provide daytime music according to patient's preference.<br>3. Administer sedatives or hypnotics as prescribed. |
| Potential ineffective family coping | Patient's sister and son will verbalize questions and feelings about sudden death, surgery, and recovery. | 1. Assess family members' level of understanding about procedures.<br>2. Begin family teaching plan. |

*Continues*

**Table 9-2**  *continued*

| Nursing Diagnoses | Expected Outcomes | Interventions |
|---|---|---|
| | | 3. Provide family members with a copy of patient/family AICD manual. |
| Knowledge deficit | Patient will verbalize need for procedure and postoperative rehabilitation plan. | 1. Develop teaching with patient, to include<br>• need for AICD<br>• ICU procedures<br>• need for postoperative ambulation and chest physiotherapy |

The patient had a strong family history of early coronary artery disease. She had hypertension but was taking no medication. She was divorced, lived alone, and worked full time. Her sister and son accompanied her to the hospital.

Records from the referring hospital detailed her recent medical history. On December 4th, Mrs. B. developed syncope at home and was discovered by her son, who called the paramedics. Her electrocardiogram at that time showed supraventricular tachycardia, and she was taken to a local hospital for treatment of congestive heart failure. During this hospitalization she developed nonsustained ventricular tachycardia, which responded to administration of intravenous lidocaine. She was discharged on oral encainide 7 days later.

On December 20th, the patient developed ventricular tachycardia that did not respond to intravenous lidocaine. She was subsequently rushed to the emergency department and converted to normal sinus rhythm with a 25-joule countershock. An intravenous infusion of procainamide was started at 3 mg/min. Oral verapamil and amiodarone were also started. Two days later, the patient was transferred to the referral hospital for further evaluation and electrophysiological studies.

One day after admission to the referral hospital, Mrs. B. developed ventricular tachycardia that was not converted with a 25-joule countershock. Instead, ventricular fibrillation occurred. The ventricular fibrillation was converted to normal sinus rhythm with a 400-joule countershock. The procainamide was stopped, and intravenous lidocaine was started at 3 mg/min. The following day, December 24th, a bedside multigated acquisition (MUGA) scan revealed a dilated left ventricle with an apical aneurysm. The ejection fraction was 38%. The immediate diagnostic plan included left- and right-sided heart catheterization and electrophysiological studies.

On December 26th, the patient had two additional episodes of ventricular tachycardia. During the first episode, a 100-joule shock was delivered by an intracardiac pacing catheter. It did not terminate the dysrhythmia. A second shock of 200 joules restored normal sinus rhythm. There was signifcant occlusion of the right coronary artery, and elevated pulmonary capillary wedge pressures during the first episode of ventricular tachycardia. Medications at this time were amiodarone, 1800 mg/day orally; bretylium, intravenously at 2 mg/min; and lidocaine, intravenously at 3 mg/min. Later that day, a two-dimensional echocardiogram revealed severe mitral regurgitation and a right ventricular infarction.

Mrs. B. remained in normal sinus rhythm for 5 days. During this period, the lidocaine and bretylium infusions were weaned. Oral amiodarone was continued as members of the health care team began discussing her need for cardiac surgery and possible implantation of an AICD. Her primary nurse coordinated her preoperative preparation and discussed her anxieties with the pyschologist and her family in order to develop a consistent approach to support her coping. Social services were consulted to help Mrs. B. with her concerns about her insurance coverage and to provide support to her sister and son.

On January 8th, a bypass graft to the right coronary artery and a mitral annuloplasty were performed. An AICD was also implanted. Her postoperative course was marked by bleeding and two episodes of ventricular tachycardia. Within the first 24 hours, the bleeding was controlled without reoperation. Both episodes of ventricular tachycardia were converted to normal sinus rhythm following 26-joule pulses from the AICD. The following morning, Mrs. B. was successfully extubated. By January 11th, all invasive lines were removed. Her chest, abdominal, and leg wounds were healing well. Mrs. B.'s acute needs in the immediate postoperative period were

- potential decreased cardiac output due to bleeding and ventricular arrhythmias
- potential impaired gas exchange due to postoperative atelectasis
- impaired verbal communication due to endotracheal intubation
- impaired skin integrity due to surgical incisions
- potential for infection due to surgical incisions and invasive lines
- alteration in comfort: pain
- sleep deprivation due to ICU environment and routine
- potential ineffective family coping
- knowledge deficit.

A standardized protocol helps the health care team deal with such a long problem list.

## Long-term Phase Follow-up

After the initial recovery phase, the care plan focuses on the patient's emotional stability in coping with the implanted device. Teaching programs about the specifics of device operation are a priority for the patient, family members, and community emergency services near the patient's home.[12] Support groups may be available for patients and their families in metropolitan areas.

### Case Study: continuation

Prior to discharge, Mrs. B.'s comprehensive patient care plan focused on preparing Mrs. B. and her family to deal with AICD malfunction. An education plan was prepared by the nurse from the electrophysiology laboratory. Community resources were contacted to provide additional support to both Mrs. B. and her family. Her son and sister attended basic cardiopulmonary resuscitation (CPR) training. They also arranged a schedule to alternate living in Mrs. B.'s house after her discharge from the hospital.

**Table 9-3** Pre-discharge Comprehensive Patient Care Plan

| Nursing Diagnoses | Expected Outcomes | Interventions |
|---|---|---|
| Potential for injury due to possible AICD malfunction | AICD will discharge during future episodes of ventricular tachycardia. | 1. Provide instructions about unnecessary shocks:<br>• 1 = call physician<br>• 2 = call physician and probable Holter monitor<br>• 3 or more = call paramedics<br>2. Obtain Medic-Alert bracelet and pocket identification card.<br>3. Check pre-discharge chest x-ray film to visualize lead placement.<br>4. Schedule clinic visits every 2 months to check battery and number of shocks delivered. |
| Anxiety and powerlessness due to feelings of dependency on AICD | Patient will verbalize feelings about AICD during rehabilitation phase and during follow-up visits. | 1. Provide time for patient to express fears and feelings.<br>2. Arrange consultation for patient and family with team psychologist. |
| Potential activity intolerance due to excessive AICD firing caused by increased heart rate with exercise | Heart rate is within preset limits with normal activities and exercise. | 1. Prescribe exercise treadmill testing prior to discharge ($\beta$-adrenergic blocker may be prescribed to control ventricular rate response). |

Mrs. B. expressed anxiety about her dependency on the AICD. She was also apprehensive about her allowed activity level. A progressive cardiac rehabilitation schedule was started in the hospital. Life-style changes, activity limitations, and pre-discharge diagnostic tests were discussed with Mrs. B. and her family. Pre-discharge care is described in Table 9-3.

## REFERENCES

1. Mirowski M: The automatic implantable cardioverter-defibrillator: An overview. *J Am Coll Cardiol* 1985;6:461–466.

2. Mirowski M, Mower MM, Reid PR, Watkins L, Langer A: The automatic implantable defibrillator—new modality for treatment of life-threatening ventricular arrhythmias. *PACE* 1982;5:384–401.

3. *AICD Physicians Manual.* St. Paul, MN, Cardiac Pacemakers, 1985.

4. Cobb L, Werner J: Predictors and prevention of sudden cardiac death, in Hurst JW: *The Heart, Arteries, and Veins,* ed 6. New York, McGraw-Hill Book Co, 1986, pp 538–545.

5. Purcell JA, Jedamski BA: Prognosis of patients with persistent ventricular arrhythmias following myocardial infarction. *Prog Cardiovasc Nurs* 1987;2:23–31.

6. Walton J: Identification of patients at high risk for sudden cardiac death. *Focus Crit Care* 1987;14(6):70–75.

7. Douglas MK: The use of electrophysiologic studies in the management of recurrent ventricular tachyarrhythmias, in Douglas MK, Shinn JA (eds): *Advances in Cardiovascular Nursing.* Rockville, MD, Aspen Publishers, 1985.

8. Zimmaro DM: Catheter ablation of ventricular tachycardia and related nursing interventions. *Crit Care Nurse* 1987;7(4):20–28.

9. Flores BT, Hildebrandt M: The automatic implantable defibrillator. *Heart Lung* 1984;13:608–613.

10. Cannom DS, Winkle RA: Implantation of the automatic implantable cardioverter-defibrillator (AICD): Practical aspects. *PACE* 1986;9:793–809.

11. Cooper DK, Valladares BK, Futterman LG: Care of the patient with the automatic implantable cardioverter-defibrillator: A guide for nurses. *Heart Lung* 1987;16:640–648.

12. Noel DK, Burke LJ, Martinez B, Petrie K, Stack T, Cudworth KL: Challenging concerns for patients with automatic implantable cardioverter-defibrillators. *Focus Crit Care* 1986;13(6):50–58.

**RECOMMENDED READING**

Barbola J, Denes P, Ezri MD, Hauser RG, Serry C, Goldin MD: The automatic implantable cardioverter-defibrillator: Clinical experience, complications, and follow-up in 25 patients. *Arch Intern Med* 1988;148:70–76.

Bryant JM, Pardoe P, Riegel BJ: Care of the patient with an automatic implantable cardioverter-defibrillator, in Riegel BJ, Dreifus LW (eds): *Dreifus's Pacemaker Therapy: An Interprofessional Approach*. Philadelphia, FA Davis Co, 1986.

Fisher JD, Furman S: Automatic implantable cardioverter-defibrillator: Patient survival, battery longevity and shock delivery analysis. *J Am Coll Cardiol* 1987;9:1349–1356.

Guarnieri T, Levine JH, Veltri EP, Griffith LSC, Watkins L, Jaunteguy J, Mower MM, Mirowski M: Success of chronic defibrillation and the role of antiarrhythmic drugs with the automatic implantable cardioverter/defibrillator. *Am J Cardiol* 1987;60:1061–1064.

Moser SA, Crawford D, Thomas A: Caring for patients with implantable cardioverter-defibrillators. *Crit Care Nurs* 1988;8(2):52–64.

Mower MM, Reid PR, Watkins L, Griffith LS, Platia EV, Bach SM, Imran M, Jaunteguy JM, Mirowski M: Automatic implantable cardioverter-defibrillator structural characteristics. *PACE* 1984;7:1331–1337.

Nisam S: Automatic implantable cardioverter-defibrillator (AICD)—A clinical and technical review. *J Med Eng Technol* 1987;11(3):97–102.

Sharma AD, Guiraudon G, Klein GJ, Yee R: A Canadian hospital's experience with the automatic implantable cardioverter/defibrillator. *Can Med Assoc J* 1987;137:809–815.

Stack JM, Houston C, Mirowski M, Mower M, Watkins L, Reid PR: Automatic implantable defibrillator for the patient with recurrent refractory malignant ventricular arrhythmias: Case report. *Heart Lung* 1982;11:512–515.

Valladares BK, Lemberg L: A new device for the prevention of sudden death. *Heart Lung* 1985;14:632–635.

Valladares BK, Lemberg L: Problem solving for complications with the AICD. *Heart Lung* 1987;16:105–108.

# Cardiac Assist Devices

*Richard A. Henker and Danni Brown*

# 10

A variety of mechanical cardiac assist devices are being used in the care of patients with severe heart failure. Clinical trials will determine which patients will benefit most from the use of these devices. The mechanical assist devices will be modified and improved as greater experience is gained. In this chapter the following devices are discussed: pulmonary artery balloon pumping, ventricular assist devices, and the total artificial heart. Common cardiac assist devices are listed in Table 10-1.

## PULMONARY ARTERY BALLOON PUMPING

The use of pulmonary artery balloon pumping has received little attention despite the need for treatment of severe right ventricular failure. This procedure is used in patients following a Fontan procedure, in patients with right ventricular hypertrophy, and in patients with refractory right ventricular failure.

The device allows the right side of the heart to pump against a lower pulmonary vascular resistance. The goal of pulmonary artery balloon pumping is to decrease the afterload on the right side of the heart. This reduction in afterload decreases myocardial oxygen consumption.

### Counterpulsation

Balloon counterpulsation is more commonly used to assist the left ventricle (the intra-aortic balloon pump). The principles of counterpulsation can be used to assist a failing right ventricle as well as a failing left ventricle.

**Table 10-1**  List of Commercially Available Cardiac Assist Devices

| Type of Device | Manufacturer | Model | Characteristics |
|---|---|---|---|
| Balloon counterpulsation | Datascope | 90 | |
| | Hoek Loos | | |
| | Kontron | 10 | |
| | Mansfield | 1300i | |
| Ventricular assist devices | Abiomed | BVS System 5000 | Pulsatile, right & left, external |
| | Biomedicus | | Nonpulsatile, right & left, centrifugal pump |
| | Elecath | | Pulsatile, external |
| | Novacor | Novacor VA System | Pulsatile, left (only), internal |
| | Sarns/3M | | Nonpulsatile, right & left, centrifugal pump |
| | Symbion | Acute VAD | Pulsatile, right & left, external |
| | Thermedics | Heartmate | Pulsatile, internal |
| | Thoratec | Pierce-Donachy | Pulsatile, right & left, external |
| Total artificial heart | Pennsylvania State University | Penn State Heart | Pulsatile, internal |
| | Symbion | Jarvik-7 70 & 100 | Pulsatile, internal |

Counterpulsation increases cardiac output by lowering afterload. Just prior to systole, the balloon deflates, lowering resistance in the cardiac output outflow tract (pulmonary artery or aorta). This lowered resistance to ventricular ejection decreases the work of the ventricle, thus decreasing myocardial oxygen consumption. Balloon counterpulsation promotes blood flow and tissue perfusion during diastole by inflating and displacing blood forward, at a greater pressure, through the pulmonary or systemic vascular systems.[1]

## Right Ventricle

The right ventricle of the heart is designed for low pressure pumping. This matches the lower resistance of the pulmonary circuit.[1] The right ventricle has a relatively thin wall (4 to 5 mm compared with 8 to 15 mm on the left) and is crescent shaped. This anatomical structure accommodates lower pressures present in the normal pulmonary circulation.

The right ventricle is anterior to the left ventricle within the mediastinum. This position decreases protection of the right ventricle during cardiac surgery. This occurs because of decreased exposure to the cardioplegia solution and increased exposure to operating room lights.

## Pathophysiology of Right Ventricular Failure

The differentiation between right and left ventricular failure is important because of significant differences in treatment modalities for each.[2] Symptoms of right ventricular failure include

- jugular venous distention
- positive hepatojugular reflux
- hepatomegaly
- splenomegaly
- ascites
- nausea, vomiting, and indigestion
- abdominal distention
- peripheral and sacral edema.[3]

The causes of right ventricular failure include right ventricular infarction, left ventricular failure, pulmonary hypertension, and congenital abnormalities. Eventually the effects of single ventricular failure, either right or left, lead to biventricular failure.[4]

## Experimental Studies in Pulmonary Artery Balloon Pumping

The first studies using counterpulsation in the pulmonary artery were done in 1970. The study involved an animal model with right ventricular failure due to induced pulmonary embolism. This study showed a significant decrease in right atrial pressure and pulmonary vascular resistance when pulmonary artery balloon counterpulsation was used. This led to improved arterial pressure and improved cardiac output.[5]

Later animal studies have shown that pulmonary artery counterpulsation can improve right ventricular failure and increase cardiac output. The animal models included a series in which right ventricular hypertrophy with pulmonary hypertension was created[6] and a series in which a Fontan procedure was performed.[7] In both series, the use of pulmonary artery counterpulsation was considered beneficial.

## Clinical Studies

In the clinical trials to date, the placement of the pulmonary artery balloon pump has been limited to post–cardiac surgery patients.[8-10] The indication for these patients was the inability to wean from cardiopulmonary bypass despite the use of more conventional methods such as intra-aortic balloon pumping, inotropes, and vasodilators. Placement of the balloon catheter in the pulmonary artery is diagrammed in Figure 10-1. In none of the trials reported was a ventricular assist device used.

Cardiac surgery patients are at high risk for right ventricular ischemia postoperatively due to the previously mentioned anatomical considerations and the fact that right coronary artery lesions limit the distribution of cardioplegia solution to the right ventricle. The use of pulmonary artery balloon pumping may prove to be an important adjunct to patients in right ventricular failure.

## Future Uses

Heart failure frequently involves both left ventricular failure and right ventricular failure. Current treatments for left ventricular failure are successful, thus uncovering the right ventricular component of failure. Pulmonary artery balloon counterpulsation will be one therapy that may be employed in the management of acute postoperative right ventricular dysfunction.

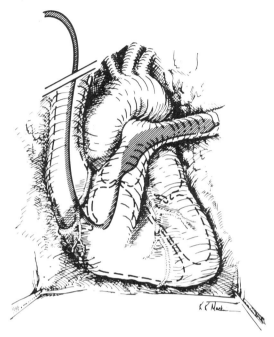

**Figure 10-1** Placement of a counterpulsation balloon in the pulmonary artery. *Source:* Reproduced by permission from *Comprehensive Intra-Aortic Balloon Pumping* by SJ Quaal, The CV Mosby Company, St. Louis, Copyright ©1984.

## Nursing Implications

Patients with pulmonary artery counterpulsation frequently have suboptimal cardiac output. Decreased cardiac output leads to tissue hypoperfusion. Hypoperfusion results in cellular hypoxia and lactic acid production and accumulation. Depending on the degree of hypoperfusion, the body may not be able to buffer the increased metabolic acid load, resulting in metabolic acidosis.

Decreased perfusion affects organ function, especially the kidneys. Altered renal perfusion may result in acute renal dysfunction. Complications of the pulmonary artery balloon pumping include

- thrombus formation and pulmonary emboli
- increased pulmonary vascular resistance

- decreased cardiac output
- hypoxemia.

The patient is also at risk for bleeding abnormalities. If heparin is used, the nurse monitors the partial thromboplastin time (PTT) or the activated clotting time (ACT). Thrombocytopenia may occur due to mechanical trauma to the platelets.

## VENTRICULAR ASSIST DEVICES

The use of the ventricular assist device (VAD) is becoming a regular part of therapy at cardiothoracic surgery centers and is no longer exclusive to large research institutions. The nurse caring for cardiac surgery patients can anticipate caring for a patient with a VAD. These devices enable the patient the time needed to recover from reversible injury to the heart.

### Clinical Indications for Placement

Among the most frequent users of VADs are patients who are difficult to wean from cardiopulmonary bypass, patients who have had a myocardial infarction, and patients awaiting a human donor heart for transplantation.

Patients have difficulty weaning from cardiopulmonary bypass most frequently when the patients have been supported by cardiopulmonary bypass for an extended period of time. Placement of the VAD extends the bypass time at the end of cardiac surgery. More recently, VADs have been inserted without having the patient on cardiopulmonary bypass. This procedure decreases the complications associated with prolonged cardiopulmonary bypass time.

A less frequent indication for placement of a VAD is augmentation of cardiac output after myocardial infarction. The placement of a VAD in this patient decreases the myocardial oxygen consumption and energy needs of the heart. The VAD provides most of the cardiac output.

The third use of the VAD is as a bridge to transplantation. The VAD maintains the patient's cardiac output until a human donor can be found. The number of donor organs compared with the number of potential transplant recipients is decreasing. The need for a life-sustaining device is apparent. VADs are filling part of this need to support patients needing transplants. The other methods for a bridge to transplantation include intra-aortic balloon pumping and the total artificial heart.

## Right and Left VADs

VADs can be used to augment cardiac output for either the right or the left ventricle. Both ventricles can be augmented simultaneously. Placement of a VAD on the left side of the heart may reveal failure of the right ventricle that is not being assisted. Heart failure can be limited to one ventricle, but this is atypical. The ventricles are part of a series circuit, and the events occurring in one ventricle often affect the other ventricle. The right and left ventricles share the intraventricular septum, and many of the muscle fibers run through both ventricles.[4]

## Anatomical Placement of VADs

Placement of a VAD depends on the desired physiologic effect. If the VAD inflow cannula is placed in the atrium, preload is shunted past the compromised ventricle. The blood then reenters the circulation through a cannula into the ascending or descending aorta (for a left VAD) or the pulmonary artery (for a right VAD). Diverting preload decreases the myocardial oxygen consumption.

According to the Frank-Starling law, an increase in preload causes an increase in contractile force. A decrease in contractile force decreases the myocardial oxygen requirements. Therefore, the supply of oxygen to the myocardium can better meet the oxygen demands, minimizing myocardial ischemia.

Placement of the VAD inflow cannula in the apex of the ventricle will reduce afterload. The inflow cannula of the VAD provides an additional outflow tract for blood to be ejected from the compromised ventricle. This second outflow tract in the ventricle enables blood to be ejected against less resistance, thus decreasing the myocardial oxygen consumption.

A rise in afterload in the cardiovascular system requires an increase in the force with which the myocardium must contract. Decreasing the afterload decreases the amount of contractile force needed to eject blood from the ventricle. The myocardial oxygen demands will decrease with a decrease in the afterload in the ventricle. Therefore, the VAD not only augments the cardiac output but also decreases myocardial oxygen consumption by decreasing afterload.

### Pulsatile versus Nonpulsatile Flow

VADs are classified by the type of flow that they produce. Flow is either pulsatile or nonpulsatile. The nonpulsatile flow devices are used to divert blood from the atrium to the aorta (or the pulmonary artery) thus reducing ventricular preload. The nonpulsatile assist devices will produce a continuous flow of blood, resulting in a mean pressure. The pressure waveform tracings with nonpulsatile flow differ from nonassisted pressure waveforms. There is a decreased pulse pressure. The more the assist device controls the cardiac output, the narrower the pulse pressure in the waveform (Figure 10-2). A nonpulsatile flow of blood is not the physiological norm for the body. An intra-aortic balloon is frequently used to provide a pulse when a nonpulsatile VAD is used (Figure 10-3).

Pulsatile flow of blood is the physiological norm for the body. In a study by Bregman,[11] the following effects were identified in patients receiving pulsatile flow during cardiopulmonary bypass:

- increased urine output
- minimized neurologic complications
- decreased peripheral vascular resistance
- minimal subendocardial ischemia
- reduced perioperative myocardial infarction
- decreased need for inotropic support
- decreased cooling and rewarming time.

### Modes of Assistance

A variety of methods are used to trigger pulsatile VADs. The trigger events are classified as asynchronous or synchronous. If the trigger event is synchronous, it indicates that blood is ejected from the VAD in coordination with the heart's ejection of blood. The

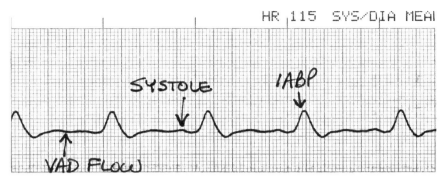

**Figure 10-2** Arterial line tracing in a patient showing laminar flow from ventricular assist device, minimal pulse with systole, and pulse from intra-aortic balloon pump.

VAD ejection is coordinated with the ECG. The ejection occurs during diastole to provide diastolic augmentation. During systole, the VAD fills, providing a decrease in afterload.

The asynchronous VAD is set at its own rate. The trigger event is usually the volume of blood in the VAD. If the VAD fills to 70 ml, it ejects the blood. Occasionally both ECG and blood volume are used to trigger the VAD.

### Patient Anticoagulation

The methods and degree of anticoagulation in patients with VADs vary. Patients are anticoagulated with heparin, dipyridamole, aspirin, warfarin, or dextran to prevent clot formation. High blood flow through the VAD decreases the risk of clot formation, and therefore the need for heparinization is decreased. At times, during maximal flow anticoagulation may not be used. The phase in which anticoagulation is most important is while the patient is being weaned from mechanical assistance. During weaning, flow through the VAD is decreased. Decreased flow predisposes the patient to clot formation.

The patient who is excessively anticoagulated has a potential for bleeding in the gastrointestinal tract and the central nervous system. The activated clotting time, partial thromboplastin time, prothrombin time, and platelet count are the laboratory values used to monitor the degree of anticoagulation in patients with VADs.

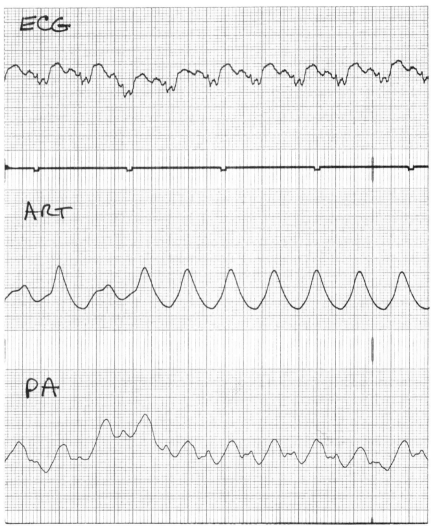

**Figure 10-3** Multiple channel recording in patient with left ventricular assist device showing electrocardiogram, arterial pressure wave with pulse due to intra-aortic balloon, and pulmonary artery pressure wave.

## Clot Formation in the VAD

Thrombus formation in patients receiving some form of mechanical assistance is common. Turbulent flow, stasis, and injury to blood components promote thrombus formation.[12] Johnston and associates described the effects of surface injury from shear stress.[13] The damage to the platelets is not significant unless they start to aggregate and release serotonin. These events trigger the formation of a clot. Hardwick and associates suggest that the exposure of the blood components to artificial valves and to extracorporeal circulatory devices can cause damage to the structure of platelets and result in thrombus formation.[14] Hung and associates determined that it takes ten times the pressure to cause red cell damage as it does to damage platelets.[15] The most frequently used method to determine red cell destruction is plasma-free hemoglobin. The plasma-free hemoglobin level may be used as an indirect measure of platelet damage.

## Potential for Infection

The risk of infection in the patient with a mechanical cardiac assist device occurs because of the patient's debilitated state, destruction of white blood cells, and/or risks of infection associated with the device itself.[16] The inflow and outflow cannulas to the VAD are potential sites for infection. The cannulas communicate with the skin and the external environment. In patients using the VAD as a bridge to transplantation, it is essential that they remain infection free.[17]

## Decreased Tissue Perfusion

If VADs, in combination with the patient's heart, do not provide adequate cardiac output, there will be a decrease in tissue perfusion. The decreased perfusion leads to end-organ dysfunction. To measure adequacy of perfusion, the skin can be assessed, the systemic vascular resistance and pulmonary vascular resistance can be calculated, and the urine output can be measured.[18] Toe temperature may be a useful index to peripheral perfusion.[19,20] The proper application of the skin temperature probe to the great toe is shown in Figure 10-4.

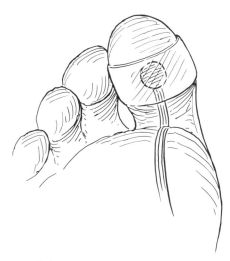

**Figure 10-4** Placement of skin temperature probe on great toe. *Source:* Reprinted from *Essentials of Critical Care Nursing* (p 126) by JM Clochesy, Aspen Pulishers Inc, Copyright ©1988.

The kidneys are a major concern in the patient with a VAD. The decreased perfusion before VAD insertion commonly causes a decrease in renal function. Toxic side effects from the VAD, such as the plasma-free hemoglobin that is produced from red blood cell destruction, lead to impaired renal function.[21] Renal function must be maximized in patients waiting for a human donor heart in anticipation of the nephrotoxic effects of the immunosuppressant cyclosporine.[17]

## THE TOTAL ARTIFICIAL HEART

The total artificial heart (TAH) is being used primarily as a bridge to transplantation. The TAH is a possible alternative because of the limited availability of donor hearts.[22] Patients who qualify for use of the TAH for transplantation include those who experience acute rejection after receiving a heart transplant and transplant candidates whose condition deteriorates rapidly while awaiting a human heart. In both of these situations, the TAH can sustain circulation until a human donor heart is obtained.

The TAHs in clinical use are pneumatically driven mechanical devices. They consist of two hemispheric ventricles that are made of polyurethane with a flexible pumping diaphragm and tilting disc valves. The inner lining is manufactured without seams (Figure 10-5). Dacron grafts are used to connect the patient's pulmonary artery and aorta to the TAH. Atrial cuffs connect the remnant atria to the polyurethane ventricles. During surgery, the Dacron grafts and atrial cuffs are sutured into position. The ventricles are then snapped into place with "quick connects."[23] With every contraction, air inflates the diaphragm in each ventricle. The diaphragm pushes the blood out of the ventricles.[23]

The TAH has been used in a variety of patients. In the early stages of use, the TAH was implanted as a permanent device for those patients not eligible for a human heart transplant. Because of the frequent embolic side effects, the TAH is currently used on a temporary basis only. The use of the TAH as a bridge to transplantation will improve organ perfusion, thus improving the candidate's overall condition.

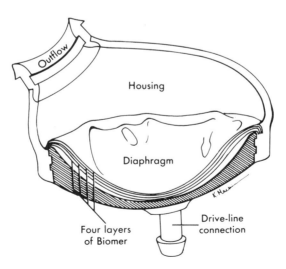

**Figure 10-5** Ventricle of Jarvik-7 Total Artificial Heart. *Source:* Reproduced by permission from *Comprehensive Intra-Aortic Balloon Pumping* by SJ Quaal, The CV Mosby Company, St. Louis, Copyright ©1984.

## Surgical Placement of the Jarvik-7

The goal of the surgical procedure is to obtain the best possible fit of the TAH in the recipient's chest. Most of the native ventricles are removed during the procedure; the atria and a small portion of the ventricles are left in place. This enables the surgeon to have more control over where the TAH will be positioned in the chest. The patient's valves are removed and will be replaced with Medtronic-Hall valves in the Jarvik-7.[24] A good fit in the chest promotes venous return and filling in the TAH. The TAH is a preload dependent device. As preload drops, cardiac output decreases.[25]

After the surgeon removes the native ventricles, the atrial cuffs are sewn to the right and left atria. The Dacron grafts are then attached to the remnant aorta and pulmonary artery. Grafts that are too long or too short place stress on the suture line, which can result in bleeding from the anastomoses.[24]

Next, the ventricles are snapped into place with the "quick connects" located on each of the ventricles and the Dacron grafts. Air is removed from the ventricles and the system gradually weaned onto the patient. Initially, the heart rate is 40 beats per minute with low drive pressures. As the heart takes more of the work from the cardiopulmonary bypass pump, the heart rate and drive pressures are increased.[24] Eventually, the patient becomes totally dependent on the TAH for cardiac output.

Right and left atrial pressures are used for initial patient monitoring. The Cardiac Output Monitoring and Diagnostic Unit (COMDU) software and computer used with the Jarvik-7 enable the TAH team to monitor cardiac output and filling volumes on a beat-to-beat basis.[25] The effects of numerous interventions on cardiac output are monitored while the patient has the TAH in place.

## Hemodynamics

The COMDU enables continuous assessment of filling volumes and the pressures that eject the blood from the polyurethane ventricles. By evaluating the waveforms representing filling and ejection, members of the TAH team can make assessments about fluid status and flow in the ventricles.

The TAH's ability to increase cardiac output with an increase in preload can be studied with COMDU waveforms. Settings on the drive system can be adjusted to maintain the Frank-Starling law in the TAH patient. The major principle used when analyzing the waveforms and making drive parameter changes is "partial fill during diastole and full ejection during systole." Once the heart driver is adjusted properly, the cardiac output will increase with an increase in preload.

Prevention of stasis of blood in the heart is the priority when monitoring the TAH. The ventricles are not allowed to fill completely, and blood is completely ejected during each contraction. If the TAH fills completely or the ventricle does not empty completely, stasis of blood occurs, predisposing the patient to thrombus formation. Complete filling of the TAH creates static flow in the ventricle, increasing the risk of clot formation. A study by Levinson and associates indicates that high flow through the TAH can be used to prevent clot formation.[26]

### Parameters on the Utah Drive System II

The Jarvik-7 TAH is powered by the Utah Drive System II (UDII). Its control parameters include heart rate, percent systole, drive pressure, and vacuum. The parameters are adjusted to attain Frank-Starling principles.

Partial fill is attained by manipulating the control parameters. If full fill occurs, it is necessary to first look to see if full ejection of blood is occurring. Incomplete ejection of blood is a possible cause of complete filling. If full ejection is occurring, the diastolic time can be decreased. This is done by increasing the heart rate or by increasing the percent systole. Vacuum influences the rate that the ventricles fill with blood. If full fill is occurring, the vacuum can be decreased to decrease the volume of blood filling the ventricle.

Full ejection is accomplished using the control parameters described above. If the TAH is partially ejecting blood, the amount of time in systole can be increased to allow the blood to be ejected from the heart. Systolic time is increased by decreasing the heart rate or by increasing the percent systole. The drive pressure on either the right or the left side can be increased to provide more force to eject the blood during the systolic phase.

Cardiac output is monitored continuously in TAH patients. The COMDU enables clinicians to evaluate immediate changes in cardiac output that occur as the result of various nursing and medical interventions.[27] Additionally, the effects of changes in drive parameters can be evaluated immediately.

## Thrombus Formation

Thrombus formation is the most frequent complication in patients with a TAH. Thrombi in the TAH form around the artificial valves or near the quick connects.[23] Thrombi form in TAH patients because of increased platelet aggregation, crevices in the valve flow rings, crevices in the quick connects, thrombogenicity of the device, resistance to heparin, and decreased cardiac output.[28] Damage to red blood cells and platelets from the increased intraventricular pressure can also lead to an increased potential for thrombus formation.[29] Hardwick and associates measured platelet response after shear stress was applied with a viscometer.[14] The result was increased platelet aggregation.

Complications associated with the use of the TAH have limited its use. The undesirable effects of the TAH currently limit it to use on a temporary basis. As technology improves, it may be possible to use the TAH on a permanent basis.

## Infection

The three areas at risk for the development of infection in the TAH patient are (1) sites where drive lines traverse the skin, (2) the mediastinum, and (3) the inside of the heart.[16] The drive lines for the Jarvik-7 TAH have a velour patch that is sewn into the subcutaneous tissue to provide a mechanical barrier to pathogens traveling along the drive lines. If a mediastinal infection occurs around the TAH, debridement may need to be done. Infection is a serious complication in these patients. The patient with a TAH must be kept infection free in anticipation of receiving a human heart with subsequent immunosuppressive therapy.[22]

## Bleeding

A variety of combinations of anticoagulants (heparin, warfarin, dipyridamole, aspirin, and dextran) are used for anticoagulation in

TAH patients. The most frequent combination is heparin and dipyridamole.[30] The goal of therapy is to prevent stroke from occurring while minimizing bleeding. Bleeding can be a serious problem in TAH patients following surgery.

### Renal Failure

Renal failure is usually due to a combination of hypoperfusion and plasma-free hemoglobin. Plasma-free hemoglobin is toxic to the kidneys. Hypoperfusion injury to the kidneys usually occurs before the mechanical assist device is implanted. For example, a patient in cardiogenic shock develops acute renal dysfunction.

### SUMMARY

As the technology used in mechanical cardiac assist devices improves and patient experience increases, the use of these devices will be more effective in improving patient survival. These devices provide additional treatment options for critically ill cardiac patients.

---

**REFERENCES**

1. Quaal SJ: *Comprehensive Intra-aortic Balloon Pumping.* St. Louis, CV Mosby Co, 1984.

2. Funk M: Diagnosis of right ventricular infarction with right precordial ECG leads. *Heart Lung* 1986;15:562–572.

3. Guzetta CE, Dossey BM (eds): *Cardiovascular Nursing: Bodymind Tapestry.* St. Louis, CV Mosby Co, 1984.

4. Weber KT, Janicki JS, Shroff S, Fishman AP: Contractile mechanics and interaction of the right and left ventricles. *Am J Cardiol* 1981;47:686–694.

5. Kralios AC, Zwart HHJ, Moulopoulos SD, Collan R, Kwan-Gett CS, Kolff WJ: Intrapulmonary artery balloon pumping. *J Thorac Cardiovasc Surg* 1970;60:215–232.

6. Jett GK, Siwek LG, Picone AL, Applebaum RE, Jones M, Austen G: Pulmonary artery balloon counterpulsation for right ventricular failure: An experimental evaluation. *J Thorac Cardiovasc Surg* 1983;86:364–372.

7. de la Riviere AV, Haasler G, Malm JR, Bregmen D: Mechanical assistance of pulmonary circulation after right ventricular exclusion. *J Thorac Cardiovasc Surg* 1983;85:809–814.

8. Symbas PN, McKeown PP, Santora AH, Vlasis SE: Pulmonary artery balloon counterpulsation for treatment of intraoperative right ventricular failure. *Ann Thorac Surg* 1985;39:437–440.

9. Flege JB, Wright CB, Reisinger TJ: Successful balloon counterpulsation for right ventricular failure. *Ann Thorac Surg* 1984;37:167–168.

10. Miller DC, Moreno-Cabral RJ, Stinson EB, Shinn JA, Shumway NE: Pulmonary artery balloon counterpulsation for acute right ventricular failure. *J Thorac Cardiovasc Surg* 1980;80:760–763.

11. Bregman D: Response to paper presented on pulsatile flow at the Fifth Annual Meeting of the Society of Thoracic Surgeons, Phoenix AZ, January 1979. *Ann Thorac Surg* 1979;28:272.

12. Kilgo GR, Toole JF, McGhee TB: Cerebrovascular disease and neurological manifestations of heart disease, in Hurst JW (ed): *The Heart*. New York, McGraw-Hill Book Co, 1986.

13. Johnston GG, Marzec U, Bernstein EF: Effects of surface injury and shear stress on platelet aggregation and serotonin release. *Trans Am Soc Artif Internal Organs* 1975;21:413–421.

14. Hardwick RA, Hellums JD, Peterson DM, Moake J, Olson J: Effects of $PGI_2$ and di-butryl cyclic-AMP on platelets exposed to shear stress. *Trans Am Soc Artif Internal Organs* 1981;27:192–197.

15. Hung TC, Hochmath RM, Joist JH, Sutera SP: Shear induced aggregation and lysis of platelets. *Trans Am Soc Artif Internal Organs* 1976;22:285–288.

16. Murray KD, Hughes S, Bearnson D, Olsen DB: Infection in total artificial heart recipients. *Trans Am Soc Artif Internal Organs* 1983;29:539–544.

17. Henker R, Shaffer L, Whittaker A: Nursing care of the patient with a total artificial heart. *Heart Lung* 1987;16:381–391.

18. Hall-Barnes-Brannon P, Batchelor-Towner S: Ventricular failure: New therapy using the mechanical assist device. *Crit Care Nurs* 1986;6(2):70–85.

19. Joly H, Weil MH: Temperature of the great toe as an indication of the severity of shock. *Circulation* 1969;39:131–138.

20. Henning R, Wiener F, Valdes S et al: Measurement of toe temperature for assessing the severity of acute circulatory failure. *Surg Gynecol Obstet* 1979;149(1):1–7.

21. Whittaker A: Acute renal dysfunction: Assessment of patients at risk. *Focus Crit Care* 1985;12(3):12–17.

22. Henker R, Shaffer L, Whittaker A: Ethics associated with the artificial heart. *Pulse* 1985;24(14):3–4.

23. Quaal S: The artificial heart. *Heart Lung* 1985;14:317–327.

24. Levinson MM, Copeland JG: Technical aspects of total artificial heart implantation for temporary applications (in press).

25. Willshaw P, Nielsen SD, Nanas J, Pichel RH, Olsen DB: A cardiac output monitor and diagnostic unit for pneumatically driven artificial hearts. *Artif Organs* 1984;8:215–219.

26. Levinson MM, Smith RG, Cork RC, Gallo J, Emery RW, Icenogle TB, Ott RA, Burns GL, Copeland JG: Thromboembolic complications of the Jarvik-7 total artificial heart: Case report. *Artif Organs* 1986;10:236–244.

27. Henker R, Murdaugh C, Smith R: Effects of nursing interventions on cardiac output in the patient with an artificial heart. *J Cardiovasc Nurs* 1988;2(2):56–67.

28. Levinson MM, Smith RG, Gallo J, Cork R, Emery RW, Icenogle T, Ott RA, Copeland JG: Clinical problems facing recipients of total artificial hearts as bridge to cardiac transplantation: Results of two recent patients, in Andrade ED, Brophy JJ, Detmar DE, et al (eds): *Artificial Organs: W. J. Kolff Festscrift*. New York, VCH Publishers, 1987.

29. Oiknine C: Rheology of the human blood, in Ghista DN (ed): *Cardiovascular Engineering Part I: Modelling*. New York, Karger, 1983, pp 1–25.

30. Joyce LD, Johnson KE, Pierce WS, DeVries WC, Semb KH, Copeland JG, Griffith BP, Cooley DA, Fraiser OH, Cabrol C, Keon WJ, Unger F, Bucherl ES, Wolner E: Summary of the world experience with clinical use of total artificial hearts as heart support devices. *J Heart Transplant* 1986;5:229–235.

---

**RECOMMENDED READING**

Copeland JG, Levinson MM, Smith R, Icenogle TB, Vaughn C, Cheng K, Ott R, Emery RW: The total artificial heart as a bridge to transplantation: A report of two cases. *JAMA* 1986;256:2991–2995.

DeVries WC: Surgical technique for implantation of the Jarvik-7-100 total artificial heart. *JAMA* 1988;259:875–880.

DeVries WC: The permanent artificial heart: Four case reports. *JAMA* 1988;259:849–859.

Dobbins JJ, Johnson S, Kunin CM, DeVries WC: Postmortem microbiological findings of two total artificial heart recipients. *JAMA* 1988;259:865–869.

Farrar DJ, Hill JD, Gray LA, Pennington DG, McBride LR, Pierce WS, Pae WE, Glenville B, Ross D, Galbraith TA, Zumbro GL: Heterotopic prosthetic ventricles as a bridge to cardiac transplantation: A multicenter study in 29 patients. *N Engl J Med* 1988;318:333–340.

Jarvik RK, DeVries WC, Semb BK, Koul B, Copeland JG, Levinson MM, Griffith BP, Joyce LD, Cooley DA, Fraizer OH, et al: Surgical positioning of the Jarvik-7 artificial heart. *J Heart Transplant* 1986;5:184–195.

Kunin CM, Dobbins JJ, Melo JC, Levinson MM, Love K, Joyce LD, DeVries WC: Infectious complications in four long-term recipients of the Jarvik-7 artificial heart. *JAMA* 1988;259:860–864.

Levinson MM, Copeland JG, Smith RG, Cork RC, DeVries WC, Mays JB, Griffith BP, Kormos R, Joyce LD, Pritzker MR, et al: Indexes of hemolysis in human recipients of the Jarvik-7 total artificial heart: A cooperative report of fifteen patients. *J Heart Transplant* 1986;5:236–248.

Levinson MM, Smith RG, Cork R, Gallo J, Icenogle T, Emery R, Ott R, Copeland JG: Three recent cases of the total artificial heart before transplantation. *J Heart Transplant* 1986;5:215–228.

May JB, Williams MA, Barker LE, Pfeifer MA, Kammerling JM, Jung S, DeVries WC: Clinical management of total artificial heart drive systems. *JAMA* 1988;259:881–885.

# Continuous Ultrafiltration Therapy

*Alice Whittaker*

# 11

Continuous ultrafiltration is a relatively new extracorporeal blood treatment used to control fluid and electrolyte balance in patients with acute renal failure or severe renal insufficiency. Removal of plasma water and electrolytes is a gradual process that closely resembles the kidneys' normal function. Conventional hemodialysis therapy may cause rapid fluctuations in fluid and electrolyte balance. These fluctuations are poorly tolerated by patients with cardiovascular instability or cerebral edema. Since continuous ultrafiltration is a gradual process, these rapid changes do not occur. For this reason, continuous ultrafiltration is becoming the therapy of choice for many critically ill patients.

Continuous ultrafiltration therapies are designed to be machine-free, technically simple procedures that are performed by the critical care nurse. The technical aspects and special nursing considerations in continuous ultrafiltration therapy are discussed in this chapter. Indications and special considerations for the use of each modality are reviewed.

## TECHNICAL DESIGN AND SETUP

Continuous ultrafiltration therapy does not require the use of hemodialysis machinery. Instead, the system is powered by the patient's arterial blood pressure. The ultrafiltration system has three components: the arterial and venous blood tubing, the hemofilter, and the ultrafiltrate collection circuit.

## Arterial and Venous Blood Lines

As shown in Figure 11-1, blood flows through the patient's arterial access into the arterial blood tubing. A continuous heparin infusion enters the arterial tubing immediately distal to the access-tubing connection. The arterial tubing also contains an arterial blood sampling port and an infusion port for administering intravenous fluids. Blood flows through the hemofilter and out into the venous blood line. The venous tubing contains a venous sampling port that is used for drawing system coagulation studies. An infusion port for intravenous fluid administration is also present on the

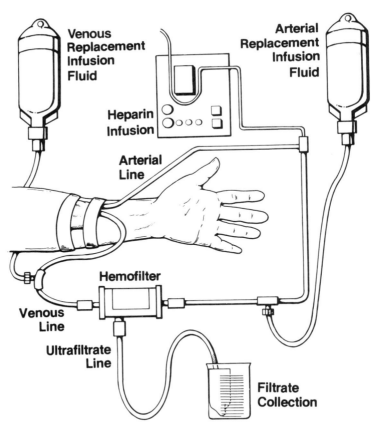

**Figure 11-1** Arrangement of components for continuous arteriovenous hemofiltration.

venous tubing. Most tubing sets also provide tubing clamps on both the arterial and venous sides.

Clinical studies indicate that long lengths of blood tubing cause increased resistance within the extracorporeal circuit.[1] Shorter arterial and venous blood lines provide minimal resistance to blood flow. Any kinking or compression of the tubing will result in decreased blood flow and possible clot formation. Utilization of short blood lines facilitates securing the tubing to the patient to prevent kinking or compression.

### Hemofilter

A number of hemofilters are available for use in continuous ultrafiltration therapies. These hemofilters are characterized as low resistance and low volume. Because the system is dependent on the patient's arterial blood pressure, the internal resistance to blood flow must be minimal. Critically ill patients may not be able to tolerate the removal of large volumes of blood used to prime the extracorporeal blood circuit. The short hollow fibers contained in the hemofilters used in continuous ultrafiltration decrease the required priming volume. The minimal priming volume of 20 to 60 ml is generally well tolerated by critically ill patients.

Hollow-fiber membranes contained within the continuous ultrafiltration filters are made from hydrophobic thermoplastic materials.[2] These membranes do not activate the complement system. They do absorb plasma proteins, which may decrease ultrafiltration rates over a prolonged period of use. The hollow fibers occasionally rupture, allowing blood loss into the ultrafiltrate compartment. The ultrafiltrate fluid should be routinely tested for occult blood. If gross blood is visible in the ultrafiltrate, the hemofilter system must be changed.

### Ultrafiltrate Collection Circuit

Ultrafiltrate collects in the external spaces around the hollow fiber membranes. The fluid is drained out of the hemofilter through the ultrafiltrate port. A collection receptacle such as a urinary drainage bag can be attached to the ultrafiltration port by a length of plastic tubing.

## DETERMINANTS OF ULTRAFILTRATION

In continuous ultrafiltration, water, electrolytes, and other non-protein bound solutes are removed as the patient's blood passes over semipermeable membranes contained in a hemofilter. The resulting ultrafiltrate is a protein-free fluid with an electrolyte concentration similar to that of plasma. The cellular components of the blood remain in the extracorporeal circuit and return to the venous circulation.

Mass transfer of water and solutes across a semipermeable membrane is a result of two mechanisms: convection and diffusion. Ultrafiltration is a convective process in which solvent (water) and solutes are simultaneously transferred across the membrane. In continuous ultrafiltration, the convective force applied across the hemofilter membrane is primarily dependent on the patient's arterial blood pressure. The higher the blood pressure, the greater the hydrostatic pressure within the system. Ultrafiltration of water and solute increases when the hydrostatic pressure within the system rises. In most patients, a mean arterial blood pressure of 60 mm Hg is required to maintain adequate ultrafiltration.

Diffusion is a conductive process in which solutes are passively transferred across a membrane. Passive transfer of solutes depends on the presence of a concentration gradient across the membrane. For diffusion to occur, the concentration of solutes must be higher on one side of the membrane than on the other. In continuous ultrafiltration therapy, a concentration gradient may be established by infusing a dialysate fluid into the nonblood side of the hemofilter.

### Blood Flow

The single most important factor in determining the success of continuous ultrafiltration therapy is maintenance of adequate blood flow through the hemofilter and circuit. Insufficient blood flow results in decreased rates of ultrafiltration and may eventually lead to clotting of the hemofilter. Blood flows of up to 200 ml/min can be obtained from external arteriovenous shunts and from percutaneous femoral catheters when the mean arterial blood pressure remains above 60 mm Hg.

Percutaneous femoral catheters are considered to provide the most optimal blood flow. Because of their more central placement, they are particularly beneficial when the patient's mean arterial pressure is 50 to 60 mm Hg. Femoral catheters do have a number of disadvantages. Use of a femoral catheter restricts patient positioning, may compromise blood flow to the affected leg, and represents a potential source of infection. Arteriovenous shunts, although providing less blood flow, are more easily stabilized and provide for greater patient mobility.

Blood flow must be considered when determining target ultrafiltration rates. Some continuous ultrafiltration modalities require a higher blood flow than others. Blood flow through the ultrafiltration system can be calculated by the following formula[1]:

$$\text{Blood flow (ml/min)} = \frac{\text{Ultrafiltration rate (ml/min)} \times \text{Venous hematocrit}}{\text{Venous hematocrit} - \text{Arterial hematocrit}}$$

Since blood flow is the most important determinant of ultrafiltration, any drop in blood pressure requires rapid identification and correction. Fluid removal rates and the amount of fluid replacement should be reassessed. Vasopressors may be used to maintain the arterial blood pressure.

## Hematocrit and Plasma Protein Level

As blood passes through the hemofilter, plasma water is removed by ultrafiltration. As water is removed, there is a corresponding increase in the hematocrit and plasma protein level in the blood on the venous side of the filter. As demonstrated in Figure 11-2, there is an inverse relationship between increased hematocrit and the rate of ultrafiltration. Likewise, increases in the plasma oncotic pressure will oppose the hydrostatic pressure, resulting in a decrease in the ultrafiltration rate. Under normal circumstances, ultrafiltration will be greatest at the arterial end of the hemofilter. At the arterial end, the transmembrane hydrostatic pressure exceeds plasma oncotic pressure by the greatest margin. As blood flows toward the venous end, filtration will continue to decrease as the plasma oncotic pressure rises. When the oncotic pressure equals or exceeds the hydrostatic pressure, filtration will cease.

Elevations of hematocrit and plasma protein levels result in increased viscosity of the blood in the venous side of the filter. Increased viscosity leads to higher resistance to blood flow through

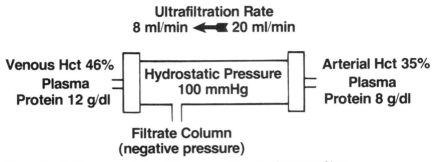

**Figure 11-2** Pressure relationships across the ultrafiltration filter.

the system. The rate of ultrafiltration will fall, and clots will begin to form inside the hemofilter. This is a frequently encountered problem in patients with acute renal failure with an arterial hematocrit greater than 40%.[3]

### Fluid Replacement

Fluid replacement requirements vary among patients and will depend on the type of continuous ultrafiltration therapy used. Most patients require fluid replacement of at least one half the previous hour's total ultrafiltrate. Significant volume depletion can occur during continuous ultrafiltration therapy. Close monitoring of the patient's hemodynamic parameters (e.g., pulmonary capillary wedge pressure, central venous pressure, arterial blood pressure, heart rate, and cardiac output) are vital to preventing fluid volume depletion. These hemodynamic parameters, physical assessment findings, and fluid balance measurements also serve to guide fluid replacement.

The type of replacement fluid administered is individualized to maintain the patient's electrolyte and acid–base status in optimal balance. The ultrafiltrate fluid contains a sodium level approximately equal to that of the blood. Normal saline or lactated Ringer's solution are the preferred fluids given to replace the sodium lost through ultrafiltration. Other electrolytes are lost in the ultrafiltrate in greater or lesser proportions than are present in the serum. For example, the sieving coefficient for bicarbonate is 1.069.[4] Bicarbonate loss through the ultrafiltrate is 6.9% greater than the level in the serum and must be replaced accordingly. The ionized fraction of calcium and plasma magnesium are two electrolytes that must be closely monitored and replaced. Failure to replace calcium and magnesium can result in cardiac dysrhythmias.

Intravenous fluid replacement can be administered through either the venous or the arterial side of the ultrafiltration system. Administration through the venous line is known as postdilution. Postdilution should be used only in patients with a hematocrit less than 45%.[5] Predilution occurs when replacement fluids are administered through the arterial line proximal to the hemofilter. There are several advantages to using predilution. Infusing replacement solution through the arterial tubing lowers the pre-filter hematocrit, resulting in decreased blood viscosity. The flow of blood through the filter is enhanced, leading to a higher rate of ultrafiltration. The potential for clot formation is diminished. Predilution also decreases the plasma protein concentration, and therefore the plasma oncotic pressure. Lowering the oncotic pressure has a significant positive effect on the ultrafiltration rate.

## Filtrate Column

Hydrostatic transmembrane pressure can also be increased by the negative pressure exerted by the ultrafiltrate fluid column. The column consists of the tubing connecting the ultrafiltrate port of the hemofilter and the ultrafiltrate collection receptacle. Each centimeter of fluid column height is equal to approximately 0.74 mm Hg of negative pressure.[6] Therefore, the longer the vertical column above the collecting device, the greater the rate of ultrafiltration. Clinical studies have demonstrated a 30% increase in ultrafiltration rate when using a 40-cm tubing column length. The rate of ultrafiltration can be adjusted by raising or lowering the collection receptacle. In addition, a screw clamp can be placed on the ultrafiltrate tubing to decrease the rate of fluid removal.

## Suction

Suction may be added to the ultrafiltrate port to increase the rate of ultrafiltration. Significant increases in filter output rates have been obtained when using suction set at 200 mm Hg. The major problems associated with suction-assisted continuous ultrafiltration are related to excessive removal of ultrafiltrate, resulting in an elevated hematocrit within the hemofilter. When this occurs, blood viscosity increases, blood flow slows, and clots begin to form. Clinical studies have demonstrated that the problem of suction-induced hemoconcentration can be diminished by the use of predilution fluid replacement.

## ANTICOAGULATION OF THE ULTRAFILTRATION CIRCUIT

The majority of critically ill patients receiving continuous ultrafiltration will require anticoagulation therapy to prevent clotting of the hemofilter and blood lines. At the same time, heparinization should be minimized to prevent bleeding in high-risk patients. Heparin requirements will vary depending on the patient's hematocrit level, the method of fluid replacement, and the presence of preexisting coagulation abnormalities. Patients with certain types of liver disease and those with low platelet counts or prolonged prothrombin times and partial thromboplastin times may require little or no heparinization.

Immediately prior to beginning continuous ultrafiltration in a patient with normal coagulation status, an initial dose of heparin is administered. This dose of 500 to 2000 units of heparin provides initial anticoagulation of the ultrafiltration circuit. Continuing anticoagulation is achieved by administering a heparin infusion through a port on the arterial blood line. The heparin infusion dosage is recommended to begin at approximately 10 units/kg/hr.[7] The patient's partial thromboplastin time (PTT) or activated clotting time (ACT) is monitored on a routine basis, and the heparin infusion is titrated to prevent inadequate or excessive anticoagulation. Changes in heparin dosage will also be required if the patient's hematocrit fluctuates or the method of fluid replacement changes. Any evidence of clotting in the hemofilter or blood lines requires immediate coagulation studies and recalculation of heparin dosage.

Although the level of anticoagulation is relatively low, the patient on continuous ultrafiltration therapy is at risk of untoward bleeding. Testing for occult blood, minimizing invasive procedures, and proper securing of all blood lines will decrease the potential for blood loss.

## CONTINUOUS ULTRAFILTRATION MODALITIES

Until this point, continuous ultrafiltration has been discussed as a single therapeutic modality. In fact, there are three variations of ultrafiltration therapy. Each of these variations is designed to meet the renal replacement needs of a specific group of patients.

### Slow Continuous Ultrafiltration

Slow continuous ultrafiltration (SCUF) is a therapy in which small amounts of plasma water are slowly removed from the patient. Fluid removal is continuous, and the therapy may continue for 1 to 3 days or longer. In most patients, plasma water is removed at rates of 150 to 300 ml/hr. Because the required ultrafiltration rate is low ($\leq$ 5 ml/min), SCUF can easily be performed using an external arteriovenous shunt.

The therapeutic goal of SCUF is to control fluid balance and prevent hypervolemia. The small volume of solutes removed on a daily basis makes SCUF unsuitable as the primary renal replacement therapy for patients with azotemia or significant electrolyte abnormalities. SCUF has been demonstrated to be highly effective in controlling fluid volume overload in patients with severe congestive heart failure. In these patients, renal function is severely compromised and may not respond adequately to diuretic therapy. Fluid removal by ultrafiltration can achieve significant preload reduction in these patients. SCUF can be used in patients with mean arterial pressures of 50 to 60 mm Hg and in those on vasopressor infusions.

SCUF is also used as an adjunct to hemodialysis in patients with acute renal failure who require large volumes of total parenteral nutrition. These patients may become fluid volume overloaded between hemodialysis treatments. SCUF can be used between hemodialysis treatments to prevent hypervolemia and decrease the need for additional hemodialysis treatments.

Although fluid removal is relatively minimal in SCUF, volume depletion can develop if attention is not paid to fluid replacement. The majority of critically ill patients receive a number of intravenous infusions containing medications and parenteral nutrition. In most cases, these preexisting infusions are sufficient to cover the fluid replacement requirements of SCUF therapy. If the patient is receiving minimal intravenous therapy, additional replacement fluid will be required to cover the fluid loss from SCUF.

## Continuous Arteriovenous Hemofiltration

Continuous arteriovenous hemofiltration (CAVH) is a renal replacement therapy in which large amounts of plasma water and solutes are removed on a slow continuous basis. Fluid removal rates average 400 to 800 ml/hr. The high ultrafiltration rates in CAVH require a vascular access that will deliver sufficient blood flow. In severely hypotensive patients, a percutaneous femoral artery catheter may be required to achieve adequate blood flow.

Because CAVH removes large volumes of plasma water, electrolytes, and metabolic wastes, it can be used as a primary dialysis modality for patients with acute renal failure. Control of fluid volume electrolyte balance is achieved through the use of large-volume fluid exchanges. Each hour's ultrafiltrate loss is replaced with sterile electrolyte intravenous solution. CAVH provides a mechanism to dilute the patient's plasma by selectively replacing solutes. For example, hyperkalemia can easily be controlled by CAVH. The ultrafiltrate contains approximately the same amount of potassium as does the plasma. Therefore, daily removal of large amounts of ultrafiltrate with a high potassium level and replacement with potassium-free intravenous solution will have the net effect of lowering the patient's serum potassium level. The amount of fluid replacement will vary with the individual patient's fluid volume status. In general, fluid replacement removal should be slightly less than the amount of ultrafiltrate removed in order to maintain a negative fluid balance. The patient must be carefully monitored to prevent volume depletion from inadequate fluid replacement. As discussed in a previous section, replacement fluids may be infused into either the venous (postdilution) or the arterial (predilution) blood tubing. The effectiveness of CAVH on removal of urea from the plasma can be enhanced by the use of predilution. It has been shown that CAVH using predilution causes intracellular urea to shift into the plasma where it can be removed by ultrafiltration.[8] This is particularly advantageous in the prevention of azotemia in patients with acute renal failure.

### Continuous Arteriovenous Hemodialysis

Continuous arteriovenous hemodialysis (CAVHD) combines the convective transport of CAVH with diffusion dialysis. Sterile dialysate fluid is infused into the ultrafiltration compartment of the hemofilter as shown in Figure 11-3. The dialysate flows countercurrent to the blood flow to facilitate diffusion of electrolytes, urea, and creatinine. Solute removal in CAVHD is superior to that in CAVH. Solutes are removed primarily by diffusion and to a small extent by ultrafiltration. Clinical studies suggest that plasma urea and creatinine levels reach a steady state after 24 to 48 hours of CAVHD treatment.[9] Electrolyte abnormalities and disturbances in acid–base balance are also well controlled.

As in standard CAVH, plasma water is ultrafiltrated in response to convective forces. CAVHD hemofilters have ultrafiltration rates that are slightly lower than CAVH hemofilters. In general, the ultrafiltration rate for CAVHD is 100 ml/hr or less. The lower hourly fluid removal rates can be replaced by specifically prescribed intravenous infusions. In many cases, adequate fluid replacement is

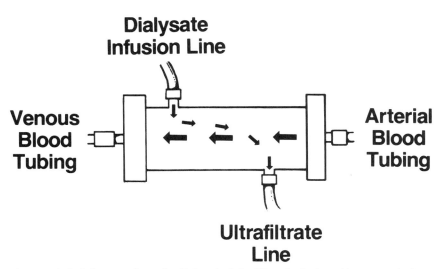

**Dialysate Infusion Line**

**Venous Blood Tubing**

**Arterial Blood Tubing**

**Ultrafiltrate Line**

**Figure 11-3** Infusion of sterile dialysate into filter during continuous arteriovenous hemodialysis.

achieved with the patient's preexisting intravenous medications and parenteral nutrition.

CAVHD has been effectively used as the primary renal replacement therapy for a wide variety of critically ill patients with acute renal failure. The ability to control azotemia and severe electrolyte abnormalities makes CAVHD an ideal treatment for extremely catabolic patients. It is well tolerated by patients with cardiovascular instability who cannot tolerate regular hemodialysis.

## SUMMARY

Continuous ultrafiltration therapy is an effective treatment for fluid volume overload and electrolyte imbalance in critically ill patients. In patients with cardiovascular instability, it is better tolerated than regular hemodialysis. The three modalities of continuous ultrafiltration allow the therapy to be individualized to each patient's specific needs. The simplicity of the technique allows the procedure to be performed by the bedside nursing practitioner.

The major nursing goal in ultrafiltration therapy is to optimize the patient's fluid balance. Nursing actions related to this goal include assessment of fluid volume status, regulation of the rate of ultrafiltration, and appropriate fluid replacement. Maintaining the patency of the ultrafiltration system is another nursing responsibility. This goal is achieved through assessment and support of the patient's blood pressure, close monitoring of anticoagulation therapy, and appropriate maintenance of the hemofilter and blood lines.

### REFERENCES

1. Swan S, Paganini E: The practical aspects of slow continuous ultrafiltration (SCUF) and continuous arteriovenous hemofiltration (CAVH), in Paganini E (ed): *Acute Continuous Renal Replacement Therapy*. Boston, Martinus Nijhoff Publishing, 1986, pp 51–78.

2. Lysaght M, Boggs D: Transport in continuous arteriovenous hemofiltration and slow continuous ultrafiltration, in Paganini E (ed): *Acute Continuous Renal Replacement Therapy*. Boston, Martinus Nijhoff Publishing, 1986, pp 43–50.

3. Olbricht C: Continuous arteriovenous hemofiltration—the control of azotemia in acute renal failure, in Paganini E. (ed): *Acute Continuous*

*Renal Replacement Therapy*. Boston, Martinus Nijhoff Publishing, 1986, pp 123–142.

4. Paganini E: Continuous Replacement Modalities in Acute Renal Dysfunction, in Paganini E (ed): *Acute Continuous Renal Replacement Therapy*. Boston, Martinus Nijhoff Publishing, 1986, pp 7–42.

5. Kramer P, Seegers A, DeVivie D, et al: Therapeutic potential of hemofiltration. *Clin Nephrol* 1979;11:145–149.

6. Whittaker A, Brown C, Grabenbauer K, Cauble L: Preventing complications in continuous arteriovenous hemofiltration. *Dimens Crit Care Nurs* 1986;5:72–79.

7. Kaplan A, Longnecker R, Folkert V: Continuous arteriovenous hemofiltration. *Ann Intern Med* 1984;100:358–367.

8. Kaplan A: The predilution mode for continuous arteriovenous hemofiltration, in Paganini E (ed): *Acute Continuous Renal Replacement Therapy*. Boston, Martinus Nijhoff Publishing, 1986, pp 143–172.

9. Geronemus R: Continuous arteriovenous hemodialysis—clinical experience. In Paganini E (ed): *Acute Continuous Renal Replacement Therapy*. Boston, Martinus Nijhoff Publishing, 1986, pp 247–254.

---

RECOMMENDED READING

Berkseth R, Kjellstrand C: Dialytic management of acute renal failure, in Glassock R (ed): *Current Therapy in Nephrology and Hypertension*. Philadelphia, BC Decker, 1984, pp 243–248.

King G: Continuous arteriovenous hemofiltration: A nursing perspective. *ANNA J* 1986;13:151–154.

Leone M, Jenkins RD, Golper TA, Alexander SR: Early experience with continuous arteriovenous hemofiltration in critically ill pediatric patients. *Crit Care Med* 1986;14:1058–1063.

Locke S, Groth N, Lees P: Continuous arteriovenous hemofiltration: An alternative to standard hemodialysis in unstable patients. *ANNA J* 1985;12:127–131.

Pacher R, Frass M, Hartter E, Woloszczuk W, Leithner C: Continuous pump-driven hemofiltration associated with a decline in alpha-atrial natriuretic peptide. *Crit Care Med* 1986;14:1010–1014.

Paganini E, et al: Fluid removal in oliguric acute renal failure using slow continuous ultrafiltration. *Crit Care Med* 1984;12:237.

Winkelman C: Hemofiltration: A new technique in critical care nursing. *Heart Lung* 1985;14:265–271.

# Closed-Loop Medication Delivery Systems

*John M. Clochesy*

# 12

A significant amount of nurses' time in the postanesthesia recovery unit and the surgical intensive care unit is spent controlling patients' blood pressures with continuous intravenous infusions. Since many of these patients have indwelling arterial catheters attached to microprocessor-based bedside physiological monitors and infusions are controlled by microprocessor-based volumetric pumps or controllers, a "closed-loop" system can be developed to automatically titrate the intravenous infusions. A control system consists of five parts[1]:

1. Patient (the controlled process)
2. Response (the measured feedback)
3. Model (the mathematical description of the process)
4. Adapter (to update the parameters)
5. Controller (to determine optimum dosing strategy.

The most frequently used drug for control of postoperative hypertension is sodium nitroprusside. A closed-loop medication delivery system is diagrammed in Figure 12-1.

Several investigators have studied closed-loop control of nitroprusside titration. The results are summarized in Table 12-1. Closed-loop titration of nitroprusside to control blood pressure was effective and superior to manual titration. Additionally, 1% of the nurses' time was spent attending to the closed-loop system compared with 18% of the nurses' time manually titrating the infusion.[4]

Success in implementing a closed-loop system for nitroprusside has others investigating other possible uses for this technology. Anesthesiologists are exploring the possible uses in neuromuscular blockade and intravenous anesthesia.[6,7] Other possible uses for

159

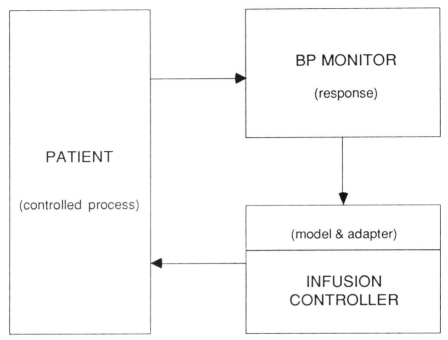

**Figure 12-1**  Diagram of a closed-loop medication delivery system.

**Table 12-1**    Summary of Closed-Loop Nitroprusside Titration

| Investigators | Sample | Findings |
| --- | --- | --- |
| Potter et al[2] (1984) | n = 10 cardiac surgery patients | Blood pressure was within 5 mm Hg of target value 75% of the infusion time and within 10 mm Hg 90% of the time. |
| Rosenfeldt et al[3] (1986) | n = 11 cardiac patients | Blood pressure was within 10% of specified value. |
| Shepherd et al[4] (1986) | n = 60; 2 groups of cardiac surgery patients | Blood pressure was closer to target for all time frames for patients receiving closed-loop titration compared with manual titration. |
| Strickland et al[5] (1986) | n = 60; 2 groups of cardiac surgery patients | Blood pressure was within 10% of target value 86.7% of the time for closed-loop group and 63.4% of the time for manual titration. |

this technology will be to titrate infusions of short-acting $\beta$-adrenergic blockers such as esmolol or labetolol. Closed-loop technology combined with the intragastric pH probe described in Chapter 3 could also be used to control nasogastric infusions of antacids or intravenous infusions of $H_2$ blockers.

---

REFERENCES

1. Vozeh S, Steimer JL: Feedback control methods for drug dosage optimisation: Concepts, classification and clinical application. *Clin Pharmacokinet* 1985;10:457–476.

2. Potter DR, Moyle JT, Lester RJ, Ware RJ: Closed loop control of vasoactive drug infusion: A preliminary report. *Anesthesiology* 1984;39:670–677.

3. Rosenfeldt FL, Chang V, Grigg M, Parker S, Cearns R, Rabinov M, Xu WG: A closed loop microprocessor controller for treatment of hypertension after cardiac surgery. *Anaesth Intensive Care* 1986;14:158–162.

4. Shepherd C, Goulart D, Rosborough D, Donovan B, Cohn L: Closed-loop Nipride therapy: A time-saving approach. *Heart Lung* 1986;15:314–315.

5. Strickland S, Jenner MH, Germann M, Pippin L, Refo J, Waller JL: Computerized infusion of sodium nitroprusside in the immediate postoperative cardiothoracic patient. *Heart Lung* 1986;15:316–317.

6. Webster NR, Cohen AT: Closed-loop administration of atracurium: Steady-state neuromuscular blockade during surgery using a computer controlled closed-loop atracurium infusion. *Anaesthesia* 1987;42:1085–1091.

7. Schwilden H, Schuttler J, Stoeckel H: Closed-loop feedback control of methohexital anesthesia by quantitative EEG analysis in humans. *Anesthesiology* 1987;67:341–347.

---

RECOMMENDED READING

Kenny GN, Rennie R, Toal F, Reid JA: Computer control of an IMED 929 infusion pump. *J Med Eng Technol* 1985;9:227–228.

Sheppard IC, Houchoukos NT: Automation of measurements and interventions in the systematic care of postoperative cardiac surgical patients. *Med Instrum* 1977;11:296–301.

# Economic Considerations of New Technologies

*John M. Clochesy*

# 13

Critical care is both capital and labor intensive. Many of the emerging technologies discussed in this book will assist in increasing labor productivity. In the current system of reimbursement, critical care is reimbursed significantly below the cost of providing the services. Either the intensity of services will be reduced or unnecessary services will be delivered to shift some cost to these later patients. Studies at tertiary hospitals indicate that thousands of dollars per patient are lost under prospective payment systems.[1,2]

## PERFORM ECONOMIC ASSESSMENT

Prior to investing in any new technology, an economic assessment must be made of current programs and practices. There is significant controversy about the cost-effectiveness of many devices and procedures. The devices continue to be employed and the procedures performed because the community standard of care has come to demand it. For legal reasons then, certain high-tech devices are used. In one study, pulmonary artery catheters altered patient management in 34% of 35 patients. Mortality was not affected by a change in therapy.[3] In other words, the patient got "the right treatment" but the outcome was unchanged. For example, in justifying the cost-effectiveness of continuous mixed venous oxygen saturation, monitoring showed an average savings of 2.65 cardiac output determinations and 5.9 venous blood gas determinations for a net savings of $75 per catheter used.[4] This savings is real only if there is no impact on revenue by the blood gas laboratory, if the blood gas technician remains equally productive, and if the number of blood gas determinations performed on the analyzer

165

does not drop below the number used to justify the capital expense for its purchase.

## DETERMINATION OF REAL COST

Traditional attempts to determine the cost of capital equipment involve the contract price and the cost of financing. Many options such as outright purchase, bond obligations, and capital leases are available. Which of these financing plans should be pursued depends on the financial situation of the institution. Often the "real" cost of a new device or technology is not known until several months after implementation. Supply costs are often a hidden cost. When replacing physiological monitoring systems in the ICU, the cost of paper used for modern digital strip chart recorders is significantly greater than that of paper used in a heated stylus recorder.

When considering acquisition of technology,

- identify realistic life expectancy based on rate of technological development in the field (when obsolete?)
- identify operating expense in terms of supplies, space, operators, preventive maintenance, utilities, and storage of output
- determine the impact on others' revenue and productivity
- determine training costs for nurses, biomedical engineers, and preventive maintenance technicians

Technologies that integrate aspects of care, increase productivity of staff, have little incremental cost of operation with increases in units of service provided, and can be kept current with upgradable software will serve both caregivers and administrators.

### REFERENCES

1. Thomas F, Larsen K, Clemmer TP, Burke JP, Orme JF, Napoli M, Christison E: Impact of prospective payments of a tertiary care center receiving large numbers of critically ill patients by aeromedical transport. *Crit Care Med* 1986;14:227–230.

2. Thomas F, Fox J, Clemmer TP, Orme JF, Vincent M, Menlove RL: The financial impact of Medicare diagnosis-related groups: Effect upon

hospitals receiving cardiac patients referred for tertiary care. *Chest* 1987;91:418–423.

3. Tuchschmidt J, Sharma OP: Impact of hemodynamic monitoring in a medical intensive care unit. *Crit Care Med* 1987;15:840–843.

4. Orlando R: Continuous mixed venous oximetry in critically ill surgical patients: "High-tech" cost-effectiveness. *Arch Surg* 1986;121:470–471.

**RECOMMENDED READING**

Bayer R, Callahan D, Fletcher J, Hodgson T, Jennings B, Monsees D, Sieverts S, Veatch R: The care of the terminally ill: Morality and economics. *N Engl J Med* 1983;309:1490–1494.

Sebilia AJ: Critical care units—responding to the changing economic climate. *Crit Care Nurs* 1984;4(2):36–37.

Warner KE, Luce BR: *Cost-Benefit and Cost-Effectiveness Analysis in Health Care: Principles, Practice, and Potential.* Ann Arbor, MI, Health Administration Press, 1982.

Yaggy D, Ellenbogen PS: The impact of changes in health care finance on critical care. *NC Med J* 1986;169–174.

# CHAPTER 14

# Technology, Ethics, and Critical Care

*Ginger Schafer Wlody*

# 14

## CURRENT HEALTH CARE ENVIRONMENT

Technological and scientific advances in health care have propelled complex ethical issues to the forefront of concern. As we have increased our ability to sustain life, we have encountered increasing ethical dilemmas. The current state of technology reveals that advances have occurred in every aspect of medical and health care. As we become more proficient in prolonging life, replacing body parts, predicting genetic defects, treating the fetus in utero, and using embryonic tissue to combat specific illnesses, we have learned that each new technology engenders a multitude of conflicts, dilemmas, and legal questions.

Since 1968 there has been a rapid increase in hospital care expenditures that can be attributed to inflation in prices of medical goods and services and a high intensity of medical care being provided to a larger population. Anderson and Steinberg describe the technological arsenal that is already in place in hospitals.[1] Technological advances, although they are awesome and provide help for many patients, also require tremendous investments of highly skilled personnel and costly equipment to support them. The number of beds in ICUs continues to increase, as does the number of admissions to ICUs. In the 1950s there were only a handful of ICU beds in the country, and today there are more than 66,000. Although ICU beds make up just 6% of total hospital beds, they account for 20% of all medical costs, an amount equal to 1% of the gross national product.[2] Not everyone believes that the focus on high technology is appropriate. One author states that the urge to employ technological interventions is a result of a "pervasive American infatuation with high technology."[3] Another writes that this conception of technological progress does not necessarily arise from a deep commitment to save human lives.[4]

Technology may be abused. For example, in one study that evaluated chart data for 382 patients with pacemaker implants it was determined that the indications for implantation were not appropriate or not documented on the basis of standard clinical practice in 20% of the patients.[5] The need to have one government body look at technology has been identified, and the Office of Technology Assessment (OTA) was created as an advisory arm of Congress in 1972. OTA's basic function is to help legislative policymakers anticipate and plan for the consequences of technological changes and to examine the many ways in which technology affects people's lives.[6] Economic conflicts occur as hospitals want to expand technology to remain competitive yet want to keep costs under control, which translates to maintaining the technological status quo.

As technology has become more complex and more intertwined with human life, and more choices are available for the health care team, ethical conflicts emerge. Use of the technology actually creates situations never before encountered. One of the greatest challenges to our society today is to address the ethical issues that arise. Decisions involving care of the hopelessly ill, transplantation, appropriate withholding or withdrawal of life support systems, and a patient's right to refuse further treatment arise and require recognition, discussion, and action.

Some of the major consequences of technology-induced dilemmas are the effects they can and do have on critical care nurses. On one hand, the critical care nurse may be bound to provide life-sustaining care hour after hour, day after day to a patient who does not respond and for whom there is no hope of response. On the other hand, the same nurse must cope with a confusing and highly charged emotional situation in which she or he constantly gives yet receives no psychological support or fulfillment.[7]

In previous chapters many new types of technological advancements in the medical field have been described. New medical technologies could fall into three major categories: devices, procedures, and organ transplantation. Examples of these three types of technological advances are shown in Table 14-1. The use of current technological advances, recent societal changes in relation to health care, and the ethical dilemmas that ensue from the use of this new technological armamentarium are discussed in this chap-

**Table 14-1**  Three Categories of Technological Advances with Examples

| *Devices* | *Procedures* | *Organ Transplantation* |
| --- | --- | --- |
| Respirator | Artificial insemination | Heart |
| Left ventricular assist device | Freezing of semen | Lung |
| Right ventricular assist device | Surrogate motherhood | Pancreas |
| Total artificial heart | (embryonic trans- | |
| | plant) | Joints |
| Pacemaker (multiple types) | Genetic engineering | Multiple organs |
| Artificial feeding devices | Fetal surgery | Cornea |
| Defibrillators (internal/ | Amniocentesis/genetic | Liver |
| external) | identification | Nerves |
| Insulin pumps | Hemodialysis | |
| | Continuous ambula- | |
| | tory peritoneal | |
| | dialysis | |

ter. Ethical dilemmas that most frequently occur in the critical care setting are identified and factors that affect them are discussed. The role of the nurse and the health care team in addressing ethical dilemmas is explored. In addition, several questions regarding ethics, technology, and the future are presented.

## SOCIETAL CHANGES

### Changing Belief Patterns

Although technological advances have occurred with great rapidity during the past 20 years, societal and cultural belief systems have not kept pace. During this time span, societal changes have occurred in attitudes toward access to care, beliefs about the infallibility of the physician, and attitudes toward death and dying, informed consent, and the handicapped. Universal access to care was a major issue in the early 1960s when the concepts of Medicare and the Great Society deemed that everyone was entitled to equal access to care. Today it seems our society is returning to the concept of limited access to care, with the patient having personal responsibility to provide for care. The phrase "equal access to care" is being replaced by "equitable access" to care.[3] Conflicts occur because the needy are unable to afford care previously deemed "their basic right." Patients who are unable to pay for care find themselves turned away or referred to other centers because of the scarcity of resources. This occurs, even though legislation has been formulated to prevent "patient dumping."

## Scarce Resources

Scarce or decreased resources have the effect of forcing those in the health care field to make difficult choices in a strained economy. As resources become scarce, harder choices will need to be made. When there are only three temporary pacemakers available and there are four patients who need them, what does the head nurse of the ICU do? When there are only a limited number of critical care beds and patients fill them, what does the nurse do when another critically ill patient needs to be admitted? "Priority utilization" will become slick bywords as we learn that there are no easy answers to these questions, merely hard choices. In the past we have always believed that if we *can* do something in health care, then it followed that we *should* do it. Today, that principle is being reexamined because of the closed pool of resources that we are facing.

## Withdrawal of Life Support/Patient Autonomy

Another recent societal change that has evolved is shown in our attitudes toward death. Technology seems to be used to prevent death at any cost, even when it is clear that the outcome is hopeless. The case of Karen Quinlan illustrates this point:

Karen Quinlan died in 1987. Just a little over 10 years previously the young woman went into a coma in New Jersey. The entire world knew of her parents' struggle to discontinue ventilator support when it appeared that the coma was irreversible. Physicians and hospital officials would not permit it. The courts decided in favor of the family, and the ventilator was removed. Karen amazed many in the medical community by living without ventilator support. After years in a vegetative state in a nursing home, the frail 89-pound woman surrendered to death. Karen Quinlan, by her illness and her death, had a profound impact on patient and family involvement in decision making affecting the terminally ill patient and the right of the patient/family to determine the type and scope of therapy for the patient.

The case of Karen Quinlan illustrates the struggle for a patient's family to withdraw life support technology. The ethical conflict is that of patient autonomy vs. paternalism. In this case, Karen's parents were acting on her behalf in trying to discontinue treatment that was of no benefit. The hospital and physician were, in essence, forcing this treatment (the ventilator) on the patient. The Karen Quinlan case was made even more complex because of her lack of ability to make decisions for herself. The question of who should make health care decisions for those who are unable to, or those who have been declared incompetent, has now been decided by the courts. Prior to 1976 the issue had not been addressed. The Barber decision discussed who can appropriately decide for incompetent patients.[8] In such cases the physician must identify a surrogate to make a "substituted judgment" on the patient's behalf. The court found that it is legal to bypass formal conservatorship proceedings, unless there is legislation to the contrary. It reasoned that a spouse and children are the most appropriate surrogates because they are in the best position to know the patient's feelings and desires regarding therapy, would be most affected by the treatment decision, are concerned for the patient's comfort and welfare, and have expressed an interest in the patient through visits or inquiries to the patient's physician or hospital staff.[9]

Recently there has been increased use of the "living will" in which patients can designate their wishes regarding life support therapy and medical care should they become incompetent to decide.[10] The living will has no binding force in some states (38 states have enacted living will or "natural death" legislation), but the document still stands as an expression of the patient's wishes.[11] The durable power of attorney for health care concept used in California has served to provide mechanisms by which patient wishes can be known, should patients become unable to make decisions for themselves during the course of an illness.[12] These mechanisms enhance patient autonomy and increase involvement in the decision-making process.

## Informed Consent

The principle of autonomy is the moral basis for the legal doctrine of informed consent.[13] The doctrine of informed consent, which also includes the right of informed refusal, has been expanded in the past 10 to 15 years. Physicians, nurses, and other health care providers are obligated to provide adequate information to the patient regarding treatment options, risk vs. benefit, and expected outcomes. The three basic requisites to informed consent include the following[14]:

1. The patient must have the capacity to reason and make judgments.
2. The decision must be made voluntarily and without coercion.
3. The patient must have a clear understanding of the risks and benefits of the proposed treatment alternatives, or nontreatment, in addition to a full understanding of the nature of the disease and the prognosis.

Nurses have a special obligation to ensure that the patient receives informed consent because it is their duty to protect the patient. The American Association of Critical-Care Nurses has taken a stand to ensure that patients have the mechanism of informed consent by publishing a position statement on *Ethics in Critical Care Research.*[15] This document supports the ethical principles of autonomy, beneficence, and justice as underlying the conduct of research in critical care units. Institutional review boards who review research protocols are now mandatory. Legislation has resulted in expanded patient protection from situations in which informed consent was limited or nonexistent.

## IDENTIFICATION OF ETHICAL CONFLICTS

Ethical dilemmas occur when a solution to a conflict encroaches on the interests and welfare of another.[16] Usually conflicts occur when two "good things" conflict with each other. For example, prolonging life may conflict with the patient's autonomy to make decisions about his or her care. Our society strongly values prolongation of life, but it also places great importance on the patient's right to decide about his or her own care.

An array of dilemmas occur in critically ill patients (Table 14-2). However, it seems that dilemmas in the critical care environment most frequently center around four ethical conflicts: autonomy vs. paternalism, duty (deontological approach) vs. outcome (teleologi-

**Table 14-2** Patient Care Dilemmas

| Dilemmas | Case Type |
|---|---|
| Withholding treatment (i.e., antibiotics) | Quadriplegia with other medical problems |
| Code vs. no code | Cardiomyopathy with severe chronic obstructive pulmonary disease; needs ventilator for rest of life |
| Right to die at home | Transplant patient |
| Technology vs. cost | DDD pacemaker vs. VVI pacemaker |
| Nutritional dilemmas | Withdrawal of food and fluids vs. tube feeding |
| Resource allocation, triage decisions | Who gets the bed? Do not resuscitate patient? |
| Technology vs. quality of life decisions | Left ventricular assist device |
| Informed consent | Patient scheduled for bilateral above-the-knee amputations vs. death |

cal approach), justice vs. utilitarianism, and veracity vs. fidelity (Table 14-3). Brief definitions of common ethical principles are found in Table 14-4.

## Autonomy vs. Paternalism

Individual freedoms are highly valued in the United States of America and are supported by our Constitution and societal norms. On the other hand, American medicine has a strong history and tradition of paternalism.[17] This causes a conflict in which patients may be pressured to use a specific technology. These conflicts occur frequently in the intensive care unit because of the highly technological environment.

Autonomy refers to the right of the patient to self-determination and freedom of choice. Autonomy asserts that humans have incalculable worth, deserve respect, and have the right to self-determination.[18] If a competent patient makes a clear statement about his or her wishes, then these wishes should be respected. Freedom of choice requires that full information be given to the patient; thus, informed consent is defined as the right of competent adults to accept or refuse medical treatment on the basis of full information.[19] The right of competent adult patients with incurable, but not im-

**Table 14-3**    Ethical Conflicts in Care of the Critically Ill Patient

| Autonomy vs. Paternalism<br>Conflicts Related to Rights of the Individual |
| :---: |
| Informed Consent<br>Technology vs. Quality of Life<br>Code vs. No-Code Decisions |
| **Justice vs. Utilitarianism**<br>Conflicts Related to Resource Allocation<br>and Triage Decisions |
| Nutritional Dilemmas<br>Qualify of Life Decisions |
| **Veracity vs. Fidelity**<br>Conflicts Related to the Unique Role of the Nurse/<br>Other Health Care Professionals |
| Withholding Therapy<br>Right To Die at Home<br>Truth-telling |
| **Professional Integrity vs. Own Ethical and Moral Beliefs**<br>Professional vs. Personal Conflicts |
| Delivering Treatment That Goes Against One's Moral and Ethical Beliefs<br>Caring for Those Whose Practices We Cannot Accept |

mediately terminal illnesses to refuse treatment, even over the objection of physicians and hospitals, was affirmed by the California Court of Appeals in 1984.[20]

Paternalism, on the other hand, claims that beneficence (doing good for others, being helpful) should take precedence over autonomy. Beneficence also involves balancing the benefit of some therapy with the burden of it. For example, in the paternalistic approach a health care worker makes a decision for the patient, saying "It's in his best interest." This type of conflict (autonomy vs. paternalism) occurs frequently in the area of technology related to treatment decisions. If a patient needs a technological therapy that the physicians view as lifesaving, but the patient views as unnatural and unbearable, he or she may make an informed decision that the benefit does not outweigh the psychological and physical costs. The patient may then refuse the therapy. Recent case law in California supports the right of the patient to make these decisions.

**Table 14-4** Ethical Principles

**Patient Autonomy**—self-determination, freedom of choice for the patient. If the competent patient has made a clear statement about his or her wishes, then these wishes should be respected. Freedom of choice requires that full information be given to the patient, unless the patient has stated that he or she does not want to have all the information. There are exceptions to freedom of choice, but these should be rare.
**Justice**—what is just or is right. A person deserves to be treated fairly and should not be discriminated against on the basis of social contribution or mental capability.
**Veracity**—truth-telling, honesty, or integrity.
**Fidelity**—do we keep our promises? As a professional nurse we promise to care for a patient to the best of our ability.
**Beneficence**—doing good for others, being helpful, considerate, and respectful of other's rights. Beneficence involves balancing the benefit of some treatment with the burden of it.
**Nonmaleficence**—the principle of "do no harm." This principle may conflict with others when treatment decisions are made.
**Deontological approach**—the "duty" involved; duties are viewed as the basis for morality. Actions are not justified by the consequences alone, but by the rightness or wrongness of the act itself.
**Teleological approach**—rightness or wrongness of an action is based on the consequences of that action. It looks at *outcome*, what the result will be.
**Utilitarianism**—the morally right thing to do is that act that produces the greatest good (for the most people or society).
**Paternalism**—beneficence should take precedence over autonomy—at least in some cases (i.e., a health care worker makes a decision for a patient saying, "It's in his best interest.").

## Case 1

Mr. H. is a 75-year-old, oriented, diabetic male. He is single, has no family, and has lived a very independent life-style until now. He has managed his diabetes well and injects his own daily insulin. However, during the past 2 years his eyesight has failed and he can no longer drive anywhere. In addition, he has had mild renal failure, which has now progressed so that hemodialysis is needed. He is in the ICU and absolutely refuses to be "attached to an artificial machine" of any kind, no matter how persuasive the arguments. The physicians, nurses, and other health care workers become very frustrated, and a struggle ensues. It is difficult, but they ultimately honor the patient's decision, and Mr. H. is transferred out of ICU.

In cases like this one that involve use of more advanced technology, such as right and left ventricular assist devices, patients are frequently so ill and so desperate that they accept the technology without question. Nurses have conflicts in that they have a responsibility to make sure that patient autonomy is supported; yet they may not understand how the patient could refuse a technology that to them is an "everyday" treatment.

## Justice vs. Utilitarianism

Justice refers to what is just or what is right. One deserves to be treated fairly and should not be discriminated against on the basis of social contribution or mental capability. Justice demands that people have an opportunity to obtain the health care they need on an equitable basis.[13]

Utilitarianism states that the morally right thing to do is that act that produces the greatest good (for the greatest number of people, or society). The current state of expensive or limited resources has forced health care leaders to review outcomes of care. Critically ill patients consume vast resources such as personnel, time, space, highly sophisticated equipment, and pharmacological products. One of the earliest studies showed that maximum therapeutic support of patients in one intensive care unit resulted in a 1-year survival rate of 27%.[21] Other studies show that most resources are used within the last few days of life. Provision of intensive care to critically ill patients ultimately has effects on other patients (the moderately ill) from whom resources may have been diverted. Therefore, clear benefit should be gained by the critically ill patient in order to justify the vast expenditures of resources. Further studies of patient outcomes are necessary in this area.

Conflicts in this area arise because some physicians and nurses want to provide every available therapy for their patient, even though the cost (psychological and financial) may outweigh the benefits or eventual outcome. Currently there is an overriding concern for the costs of health care in the United States as well as the lack of uniform availability of basic health care. Can funds more justifiably be spent on the needs of many, rather than on the needs of the few?

## Case 2

Tiffany was born mentally retarded. Her parents were disappointed, but they adapted and came to view and treat her the same as their other two children. At 2 years of age it was discovered that she was in severe liver failure. The parents took her to a well-known university medical center and sought liver transplantation. They were single-minded in the pursuit of optimal treatment for their daughter. A liver transplant was eventually done, and rejection occurred despite optimal therapeutic conditions. Tiffany's parents were devastated and insisted on another transplant. A conflict ensued between the family and the transplant team because although another liver of the same tissue type was available, there were other patients in need. One other child had a good tissue match with the available liver. The team believed that the second child should have at least one chance to have a liver transplant and made the decision not to provide Tiffany with another liver at that time.

The issues here were between justice for Tiffany (even though she was retarded) and the fairness of sharing available organs with others in need. Nurses involved in the care of these patients become very close to the patients and families and frequently are drawn into the conflicts.

## Veracity vs. Fidelity

The concept of veracity refers to truth telling, honesty, or integrity. The nurse, as a professional, has an obligation to tell the truth. Fidelity is related to trust, or to the promises we make. Professional nurses promise to care for a patient to the best of their ability. The American Nurses' Association Code of Ethics puts forth the ethical standards for professional nurses and sets the standards for a trust relationship between the nurse and the patient.[22]

Critical care nurses care for some of the most vulnerable patients in the hospital. Because the patients are so vulnerable and dependent on the nurse, the trust relationship established is strong. As the nurse carries out this trust relationship and strives to deliver safe, quality care to the patient, conflicts may arise with other responsibilities the nurse has (e.g., to perform a painful or potentially dangerous procedure). Veracity conflicts with fidelity in these situations. Telling the patient truthful information that could cause the patient distress may conflict with protection of that patient.

### Case 3

Mrs. M. is a 45-year-old business executive who is scheduled for a triple coronary artery bypass graft. She is widowed and has no children. No unusual complications are anticipated. The critical care nurse makes a preoperative visit the evening prior to surgery to assess the patient, formulate a nursing care plan, and provide patient information about the intensive care experience. The critical care nurse and Mrs. M. establish a trust relationship by the end of their hour together.

The next day the same critical care nuse is assigned to care for Mrs. M. Word comes from the operating room that complications have occurred; replacement of the aortic valve was also necessary, and Mrs. M. will be on the intra-aortic balloon pump when she returns to the ICU. The patient returns but remains critically ill; she is intubated, has periods of consciousness during which she seems extremely frightened, and is not able to communicate verbally with the nurse. As the patient's condition deteriorates, the surgeons decide to use the left ventricular assist device. They have not explained the purpose of the technological device to Mrs. M. because of her critical state. This makes the nurse very uncomfortable. What should she do?

This is a conflict between veracity and fidelity. The nurse believes the patient should be informed about the technology to be used; yet she knows that this information may upset the patient even further because of the instability of her condition. Most critical care nurses come to terms with these kinds of conflicts early in their intensive care experience and find ways to meet both ethical obligations.

## Professional Integrity vs. Remaining True to One's Own Ethical and Moral Beliefs

Conflicts between professional integrity and remaining true to one's own ethical and moral beliefs occur in various situations. The best-known examples are related to nurses participating in abortion when this procedure conflicts with their own religious and/or philosophical beliefs. These conflicts cause great personal and psychological distress and must be dealt with so that the nurse can continue to function yet maintain integrity. Nurses have traditionally removed themselves from the specific job situation in order to spare themselves the daily conflict. This becomes necessary because management cannot function in a situation in which individual nurses are saying such things as, "I don't think homosexuality is right; therefore I cannot take care of this patient with AIDS."

Nurses who are opposed to organ transplantation or various other treatments and technologies for religious or ethical reasons will need to work in alternative patient care settings.

## FACTORS AFFECTING ETHICAL ISSUES AND ETHICAL DECISION MAKING

Many factors influence ethical decision making (Figure 14-1). Before the nurse can begin to address ethical issues she or he needs to be able to identify, appreciate, and understand these factors as they relate to each patient so that they can be considered in the overall plan. Nine basic factors affecting ethical decision making are outlined here.

### Patient Needs

Are the patient's physiological needs being met even though the patient has a terminal disease? The patient's airway should be kept clear, and he or she should receive fluids/nutrition, pain medication, and basic nursing care. Does the ICU "dump" (i.e., transfer) the patient out of the unit as soon as he or she is listed as a "no

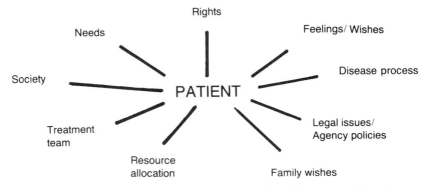

**Figure 14-1**  Factors affecting ethical issues and ethical decision making. *Source:* © 1988 Ginger Schafer Wlody.

code" or "do not resuscitate"? The family may view the situation this way: one minute the physician in the ICU is doing "everything" he or she can to preserve the patient's life and the next minute fewer and fewer resources are used. Families sometimes value care in relation to the cost and intensity of resources used, rather than what the patient needs.

## Disease Process

Which disease processes are affecting the patient? Is the disease process reversible? Is it terminal? Is it superimposed on a chronic, irreversible process? For example, does the patient have multiple sclerosis and pneumonia?

## Patient Rights

The American Hospital Association has published *The Patient Bill of Rights.*[23] Is the nurse familiar with this document? The patient should be consulted and, if possible, participate in decisions that affect his or her care. If the patient is not competent, does the next of kin or guardian have the opportunity to participate in the decision-making process? The patient has the right to privacy and to competent care and the right to informed consent regarding special procedures.

## Patient Feelings/Wishes

It is not only the patient's right to have informed consent, but it is also his or her right to have his or her wishes followed. If the patient wishes to have a living will or to be considered "do not resuscitate" and is hopelessly ill, these wishes should be honored and carried out according to hospital policy. The "do not resuscitate" order should not be rescinded by the spouse, other family member, or physician should the patient become comatose. It would seem that the only exception to this is if the patient's condition has changed in that there is a reversible element (i.e., in light of new medical information).

## Family Wishes

A major focus in recent years has been the promotion of greater patient and family participation in decision making.[24] The case of Karen Quinlan supported the conventional role of the physician and family; that is, the family decided with the advice and consent of the medically responsible individual to disconnect Karen from the respirator.[25]

Another family problem occurs in that frequently, although the patient is alert and competent, the family, or a specific member, will disagree with the patient, usually "putting the patient's feelings down" or disregarding them. This occurs especially if the patient is anoxic, losing consciousness, or handicapped. Family members, because they may have been the patient's caretakers, lose sight of the person's right to self-determination. Health care workers frequently assume this caretaker type of attitude.

The patient's family caretaker may become very fearful of the financial implications of the patient's death (e.g., a pension check will stop, and this is their only method of support). The caretaker may "need" the patient psychologically, that is, need the chronically sick person to be dependent on them. This provides the caretaker with a special role in life. It is almost as if a symbiotic relationship has developed.

## Treatment Team

The attitude of the members, composition of the treatment team, and specific specialties involved all influence the decision-making process. The treatment team is usually composed of the nurse, physician, respiratory therapist, social worker, and nutritionist. More and more often in large medical centers an ethicist, or a person who acts as an ethicist, is involved in addressing ethical dilemmas with the treatment team and family.

A nurse might consult an ethicist when there are conflicting ideas about what to do in a situation because of different values or principles (a nurse may not be sure whether to support the patient's freedom of choice or the patient's health needs). Conflicting ideas also occur with ideas of others (the nurse may believe that a handicapped infant should be allowed to die, whereas the medical resident believes that the team should make every effort to keep the infant alive). The ethicist can help the nurse clarify feelings and behave in a way that does not conflict with his or her ethical stance.

It is imperative that treatment team members collaborate. They must listen to one another and remain open to suggestions regarding the care plan. It should be the treatment team who, in conjunction with the family, decides, for example, whether a DNR patient is able to be moved to a less acute unit. Dealing with ethical issues during multidisciplinary rounds is a successful technique.

## Society

Societal changes in attitudes toward access to care, death, the handicapped, and the concept of informed consent have been discussed previously in this chapter and are all important factors that influence ethical decision making.

## Resource Allocation

Problems with funding, resource allocation, and determining priorities of care have been discussed. Resource allocation in terms of nursing staff is reaching crisis levels now during the current nursing shortage. Shortages of staff, equipment, and other resources affect the decision-making process.

## Legal Issues/Hospital Policies

The nurse must be aware not only of hospital policies related to all these issues but also the legal requirements of the state in which she is working. For example, nurses should be familiar with hospital policies on resuscitation, withdrawal of life support, care of the brain-dead organ donor, and levels of care for the terminally ill patient. Not all hospitals currently have policies in all these areas at this time, which is in itself important information for the nurse. The Joint Commission on Health Care Organizations has incorporated requirements that hospitals caring for acutely ill patients have "Do Not Resuscitate" policies in place as of January 1988.

## ROLE OF THE NURSE IN ADDRESSING ETHICAL ISSUES

Nursing has a strong tradition of ethics teaching. No decade has passed since 1900 without publication of at least one basic text in nursing ethics. The *American Journal of Nursing (AJN)*, in its first volume in 1901, published an article on ethics. In the 1920s and 1930s the *AJN* carried a regular column of nursing ethics cases.[4] Nursing curricula frequently included ethics courses until they were pushed aside after World War II by burgeoning courses in science and health care technology. By contrast, the tradition of ethics teaching in medicine is weaker. Not until the late 1970s did outside pressure result in the development of bioethics as a teaching subject in medical schools.[4] The American Nurses' Association has published a *Code of Ethics for Nurses*, and nursing schools are again beginning to offer the study of ethics as an integral part of the baccalaureate program.

Although in the past nurses frequently studied and discussed ethical issues, their stances were often based on acceptable behaviors for women in those times. Nursing carries a tradition of deference, obedience (to physicians, nursing supervisors, etc.), and loyalty.[26] In the 1970s the emerging concepts of feminism and assertiveness modified that tradition. Nursing has emerged as having a more autonomous role. Along with this autonomy nurses have developed a much stronger patient advocate role.[27] This leads one to conclude that the ethical role of the nurse is also changing. Even today, however, inherent situations exist that increase ethical dilemmas for nurses and complicate their ability to deliver optimum nursing care.

Issues that complicate ethical dilemmas for nurses include the concepts of power, control over one's actions, and role conflict. For example, nurses function under policies that are established by others; nurses are responsible for responding quickly and making split-second decisions on the unit level but have little authority or input related to higher-level decision making. Role conflicts occur, especially with physicians. This is particularly true with the more independent role of the nurse in the ICU setting.

Other conflicts that affect the nurse's ability to function well in addressing ethical issues revolve around inherent conflicts within nursing itself. For example, a conflict exists between professional models of nursing education and bureaucratic models of administration of health care institutions (i.e., education vs. service). Hence, what the student learns to think and do at the university may be frowned on in the community health care setting.

Another conflict occurs as the nurse is torn between meeting the multiple needs of the patient, the family, and physicians, all of whom may have different ethical principles, and following the institutional policies. In these days of basic cardiopulmonary resuscitation and advanced cardiac life support, it is the nursing staff that often must administer or withhold therapy. It is the nursing staff that is with the hopelessly ill patient 24 hours each day, and it is the nursing staff that is pressured by the family for information not discussed with them by the physician.

## FRAMEWORK FOR ADDRESSING ETHICAL ISSUES

In spite of the factors that create ethical dilemmas for nurses, nursing has emerged as playing a more autonomous role. In addition, the nurse is taking on greater patient advocate responsibilities. By use of a simple framework, the nurse can methodically examine ethical issues as they arise in the clinical setting (Figure 14-2).

There are three components that comprise a framework to outline the ethical role of nurses today. They are related to patients,

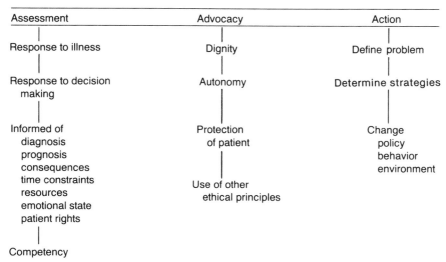

| Assessment | Advocacy | Action |
|---|---|---|
| Response to illness | Dignity | Define problem |
| Response to decision making | Autonomy | Determine strategies |
| Informed of<br>diagnosis<br>prognosis<br>consequences<br>time constraints<br>resources<br>emotional state<br>patient rights | Protection<br>of patient<br><br>Use of other<br>ethical principles | Change<br>policy<br>behavior<br>environment |
| Competency | | |

**Figure 14-2** Wlody model for addressing ethical issues. *Source:* ©1988 Ginger Schafer Wlody.

not physicians or hospitals. The three components may be referred to as the three As: *assessment, advocacy,* and *action.* These three principles provide a practical framework that nurses may adapt, based on their own system of thinking. As nurses use their own problem-solving techniques with this framework, they develop an awareness of their own values and ability to deal with various ethical situations.

## Assessment

The nurse assesses the patient's response to his or her illness in the first step of the framework for addressing ethical issues, looking at the patient's quality of life from the patient's perspective and what that quality is likely to be should therapy change. In addition to assessing the patient's response to his or her illness, the nurse must assess the patient's response and/or ability for decision making. Is the patient informed? Is he or she mentally competent? The nurse can assess the patient's or surrogate's understanding of the diagnosis, prognosis, alternatives to treatment, consequences, resources, emotional state, and patient rights. Are principles from the American Nurses' Association *Code of Ethics* being followed?[22] What about the American Hospital Association *Patient Bill of Rights*?[23] These are important aspects of the assessment.

## Advocacy

Advocacy is based on the value of human dignity, and hence autonomy. This implies the right to privacy and the right to self-determination of one's best interest. The patient (or family) must be protected from inadequate information, a single viewpoint, undue haste (or delay), coercion, lack of support, unjustified intrusion, and clear violation of his or her best interests. Nurses learn to become skilled patient advocates once they realize that advocacy is an essential component of contemporary nursing practice.

## Action

The third step in the framework for addressing ethical issues is action. The problem has been defined or located. The depth of the problem is assessed, and strategies are then determined. The nurse must decide who should initiate action, who can contribute expertise, who can contribute legitimacy, who needs to be involved, and who may be resistant to the action. For example, in protecting a patient's right the nurse may need to work to change a policy. The nurse may need to change the behavior of the family (e.g., assist them in interacting with the physician) or change the behavior of some of the other nursing staff. Nursing administrators have special obligations because of their unique professional role in the health organization. The administrator needs to be more involved with ethical issues, more supportive of staff in protecting patient rights, and more involved in development of policies related to ethics.

Another option for the nurse is to change the environment. This may consist of such action as environmental alteration or actually moving the patient to another, more suitable environment.

### Case 4

Three days prior to discharge from the navy in 1964 Mr. B. became paralyzed as a result of an intracranial hemorrhage from an arteriovenous malformation. Mr. B.

was 25 years old. In addition, there was phrenic nerve involvement, thus affecting diaphragmatic motion. After 2 or more years of rehabilitation, Mr. B. went home to be cared for by his wife. He was a ventilator-dependent quadriplegic.

Their home was modified to accommodate his physical needs. Mr. B. was alert. He and his wife discussed things, interacted intellectually, and had an active sexual relationship. At times Mr. B. would periodically require hospitalization for resolution of pneumonia or a urinary tract infection. Mrs. B. had been trained and was an expert in caring for her husband. She had become, however, a virtual slave to him in that she would not allow others to participate in his care.

In 1982, phrenic nerve pacemakers were implanted in the hope that Mr. B. might be partially independent from the ventilator. This particular hospitalization lasted 6 months, during which time Mr. B. was in the ICU. Team planning for his discharge was intense, and Mr. B. finally was discharged home to the care of his wife and visiting nurses. He was able to use the phrenic nerve stimulator to assist his breathing for a few hours during the day but still slept with the ventilator attached to his tracheostomy.

Hospitalization costs as well as an annual income that probably exceeded $2500/month were paid to them by a government agency. In 1983, the arteriovenous malformation again bled, extending neurologic damage to the C2 level of the spinal cord. Cerebral edema occurred, and the CT scan demonstrated the presence of a hemorrhagic process. The bleeding stopped without surgical intervention. Mr. B. stabilized, although his mentation was decreased, his speech capability was decreased, and he became more emotionally unstable.

His demanding behavior escalated. His wife's coping mechanisms were maladaptive. Mrs. B. became unreasonably protective and never allowed herself any time away from the hospital. Finally Mr. B. again was discharged to his home, where he improved slightly.

In June 1984, Mr. B. was admitted with pneumonia. He was again totally ventilator dependent and had a multitude of physical problems. During this time every effort was made to ready the patient to return to the home environment, but one complication after another occurred, and it soon became clear to all involved that Mr. B. was hopelessly ill. Mrs. B. insisted on staying in the ICU almost constantly. It affected other patient's families. The staff was constantly bombarded with threats by her that she would sue should her husband die. She intimidated the physicians, at times telling them what to order for her husband's care. At one point she demanded the privacy of conjugal visits, although the patient was semicomatose. Nurses actually called in sick when it was their turn to care for him, not so much because of the patient but because no one was able to deal effectively with his wife. Mrs. B. refused to acknowledge the fact that her husband would probably die.

A multitude of resources were used to assist the family. Resistant infections were treated. Total parenteral nutrition was administered when it seemed that Mr. B. was aspirating his tube feedings and his wife refused permission for a gastrostomy. Mrs. B. was given specialized attention by a clinical nurse specialist, the head nurse, a social worker, a psychiatric nurse, physicians—everyone. No one could convince her to consider that her husband was hopelessly ill and that she might consider do not resuscitate status. Mrs. B. had never really been prepared for this event and could not face life without her husband. In essence, her income too would disappear with his death.

Mr. B. became hemodynamically unstable, his level of consciousness decreased to a semicomatose state, and the sepsis continued. Mrs. B. insisted that even more aggressive therapy be initiated, and Mr. B. was transferred to a neurosurgical center with the idea that a shunt might be placed to relieve intracranial pressure. This was after almost 7 months of hospitalization. The shunt was never placed because of the patient's hemodynamic instability. Apparently during a physiological crisis at the neurosurgical center Mr. B. died.

## Discussion

What are the issues here? The use of technology conflicted with ethical principles. If the costs could be calculated, they would come to more than $300,000, or $1000/day in the ICU during Mr. B.'s last hospitalization. This does not take into account physician charges, operative charges, and the like. The question is, can our society continue to afford this in cases that are hopeless? What does the nurse do? Did the physicians in the second hospital take the responsibility to not resuscitate the patient without Mrs. B.'s permission, or did she finally accept the no code status? Could a rehabilitation nurse have helped both Mr. and Mrs. B. with this potential problem *before* the event occurred? These are questions that the nurse who is concerned about ethical issues needs to consider.

In using the Wlody Model for Addressing Ethical Issues the assessment phase occurs first. Did anyone discuss the issue of "do not resuscitate" with the patient (i.e., the point at which he would not want further therapy)? If they did, was it documented? Was there true informed consent by the patient for the procedures done? After Mr. B. became comatose of course if was not possible to ask him. Did any staff ask Mrs. B. what her husband would have wanted rather than what she wanted? What other factors might have been affecting Mrs. B.'s behavior? Were there other family members who could have participated in a family conference?

The advocacy phase is the second phase of the model. Could the critical care nurse have done anything else to act on the patient's behalf? In this particular case this is difficult to answer. However, activities the nurse performs to preserve human dignity should have been carried out. A stronger advocate perspective by the staff, rather than one based on fear and reaction to the wife, may have been the optimal approach in this difficult situation.

The action phase is characterized by strategic activities aimed at resolving the conflict. In this case when all strategies failed, an environmental change was made (necessitated by the perceived need for neurosurgery that was not available at the first hospital). This was a difficult case in which nurses faced many conflicting feelings. Ethical conflicts involved the principles of fidelity and beneficence vs. nonmaleficence. Nurses believed that continued invasive therapies were painful to the patient and that those therapies were futile.

## THE FUTURE

As costs escalate, issues related to futile technological therapy will be addressed at an increasing rate. There are a myriad of ethical issues related to organ donation and transplantation. For example, where will we obtain enough organs for those who want and need transplants? How can we avoid buying and selling of organs? Is transplantation cost-effective when compared with traditional medical therapies? Currently more than a million people receive artificial body parts each year.[28] Transplantation of fetal tissue to patients with specific illnesses has begun amid controversy. Questions such as the following may be raised:

1. How much health care technology do Americans want?
2. How much health care technology are we willing to pay for?
3. Will our pervasive American infatuation with high technology come at the expense of the elderly, disabled, and the mentally ill who need less "glamorous" care?
4. Can we accept cost containment in health care?
5. Can we, and will we, establish an equitable process of rationing?
6. Will use of increasingly complex technology continue to drive our health care system and overshadow health care efficacy and/or patient need?

Society will continue to struggle with these issues. Consumers will identify their priorities and communicate these to government leaders, religious leaders, physicians, nurses, and insurers.

## SUMMARY

The current health care environment is such that technological and scientific advances have propelled complex ethical issues to the forefront of concern. Technologic advances have leaped beyond society's ability to cope with ethical dilemmas they have induced, and nurses who have long been patient advocates are taking a more active role in assisting patients and families caught in ethical dilemmas. As the nursing role expands and becomes more complex, nurses need to be better prepared for the challenges of the future. Factors that may affect ethical issues have been discussed, and a basic framework for addressing ethical issues has been proposed in this chapter. The framework can be readily adapted to the nursing process and consists of the concepts and activities of assessment, advocacy, and action.

Nurses make a contribution by providing a climate in which patient's rights are protected and ethical issues are addressed.

---

**REFERENCES**

1. Anderson G, Steinberg E: To buy or not to buy: technology acquisition under prospective payment. *N Engl J Med* 1984;311:182–185.

2. Spingarn ND: Hospitals seek ways to make intensive care more efficient. *New York Times* 1984; June 5.

3. Richards G: Technology, costs and rationing issues. *Hospitals* 1984; June 1:80.

4. Jameton A: *Nursing Practice: The Ethical Issues.* Englewood Cliffs, NJ, Prentice-Hall, 1984.

5. Greenspan A, Kay H, Berger B, Greenberg R, Greenspon A, Gaughan MJ: Incidence of unwarranted implantation of permanent cardiac pacemakers in a large medical population. *N Engl J Med* 1988;318:158–163.

6. Hastings Center: Values, ethics and CBA in health care, in *The Implications of Cost Effectiveness Analysis of Medical Technology.* Washington, DC, Office of Technology Assessment, 1980.

7. Wlody GS, Smith S: Ethical dilemmas in critical care: A proposal for hospital ethics advisory committees. *Focus Crit Care* 1985;12(5):41–46.

8. *Barber v. Superior Court,* 147 Cal App 3d 1006, 1983.

9. Ruark J, Raffin TA, Stanford University Medical Center Committee on Ethics: Initiating and withdrawing life support: Principles and practices in adult medicine. *N Engl J Med* 1985;318:25–28.

10. Society for the Right to Die: *The Living Will.* New York, Society for the Right to Die, 1985.

11. Eisendrath SJ, Jonsen AR: The living will: Help or hindrance? *JAMA* 1983;249:2054–2058.

12. Hoffman P, Banja J: Exceptions to the right to refuse treatment. *AORN J* 1987;54:892.

13. Hastings Center: *Guidelines for the Termination of Life Sustaining Treatment and Care of the Dying.* Briarcliff Manor, NY, Hastings Center, 1987.

14.  Wanzer S, Adelstein J, Cranford R, Federman D, Hook E, Moertal C, Safer P, Stone A, Taussing H, Van Eys J: The physician's responsibility toward hopelessly ill patients. *N Engl J Med* 1984;310:955–959.

15.  American Association of Critical-Care Nurses. *Ethics in Critical Care Research.* Newport Beach, CA, American Association of Critical-Care Nurses, 1985.

16.  Levine M: Bioethics of cancer nursing. *Rehabil Nurs* 1982;7(2):27–31, 47.

17.  Harlan WR, Chianchiango D, Himes KR, Jesse MJ, Moore C, Tarazi R, Weldon CS, Buckwalter K, Molen M, Smith H: Ethics of biomedical technology   transfer:   Committee   report   on   ethics.   *Circulation* 1983;67:942A-946A.

18.  Haddad A: Ethics: Using principles of beneficence, autonomy to resolve ethical dilemmas in perioperative nursing. *AORN J* 1987;46:120–124.

19.  *Cobbs v. Grant,* 8 Cal 3d 229, 1972.

20.  *Bartling v. Superior Court,* 163 Cal App 3d 186, 195, 1984.

21.  Cullen DC, Ferrara L, Briggs B, Walker P, Gilbert J: Survival, hospitalization, charges and follow-up results in critically ill patients. *N Engl J Med* 1976;294:982–987.

22.  American Nurses' Association: *Code for Nurses.* Kansas City, MO, American Nurses' Association, 1976.

23.  American Hospital Association: *Patient Bill of Rights.* Chicago, IL, American Hospital Association, 1978.

24.  Bayer R, Callahan D, Fletcher J, Hodgson T, Jennings B, Monsies D, Sivert S, Veath R: The care of the terminally ill: Morality and economics. *N Engl J Med* 1983;309:1490–1494.

25.  McIntyre K: Recent case law and medical life and death decision making. *Ala J Med Sci* 1981;18:380–384.

26.  Kalisch B, Kalisch P: An analysis of the source of physician-nurse conflict, in Muff J (ed): *Socialization, Sexism, and Stereotyping: Women's Issues in Nursing.* St. Louis, CV Mosby Co, 1982.

27.  Murphy C: The changing role of nurses in making ethical decisions. *Law Med Health Care* 1984; September:173.

28.  Editorial: Medical report. *Glamour Magazine* 1985; June:276.

---

**RECOMMENDED READING**

Fowler MDM, Levine-Ariff J: *Ethics at the Bedside: A Source Book for the Critical Care Nurse.* Philadelphia, JB Lippincott Co, 1987.

Gilfix M, Raffin TA: Withholding or withdrawing extraordinary life support: Optimizing rights and limiting liability. *West J Med* 1984;141:387–394.

# Index

## A

Anticoagulation
for patients with cardiac
assist devices, 129
of ultrafiltration circuit,
150
Arterial blood lines for
continuous arteriovenous
hemofiltration, 144–145
Arteriovenous hemodialysis,
continuous, 153–154
Arteriovenous hemofiltration,
continuous, 152
Artificial heart, total (TAH), *12*,
132–137
bleeding and, 136–137
hemodynamics of, 134–135
infection and, 136
Jarvik-7, surgical placement
of, 134
parameters on Utah Drive
System II in, 135–136
renal failure and, 137
thrombus formation in, 136
Assist/control (A/C) mode of
ventilation, 32–33,
*34*

Automatic implantable
cardioverter-defibrillator
(AICD). 101–116
contraindications to, 106
electrodes in, 101, *102, 103*
indications for, 104–106
methods of implantation of,
106–107
models of, 102, 104
postoperative care of, 108,
*110–112*, 112–116
in acute phase, 108,
*110–112*, 112–114
in long-term phase
follow-up, 114–116
pulse generator in, 101
system of, 101–102
Autonomy
vs. paternalism, 177–180
patient, paternalism versus,
174–175

## B

Balloon counterpulsation,
121–122

---

*Note:* Pages appearing in italics indicate entries found in artwork.

Bear 5 ventilator, 43–45
Bedside monitoring, 23–27
    continuous blood gas and
        electrolyte, 23–25
    glucose continuous, 25–27
    pH, intragastric, 25–27
Belief patterns, changing,
    173–174
Bioimpedance, transthoracic,
    electrical, in cardiac output
    measurement, 75–79
Bleeding, total artificial heart
    and, 136–137
Blood flow, ultrafiltration and,
    146–147
Blood gas monitoring,
    continuous, 23–25
Blood lines for continuous
    arteriovenous hemofiltration,
    144–145

C

Cardiac assist devices, 121–137
    artificial heart as, 122,
        132–137. See also
        Artificial heart, total
    pulmonary artery balloon
        pumping as, 121–126. See
        also Pulmonary artery
        balloon pumping
    ventricular, 122, 126–132.
        See also Ventricular assist
        devices
Cardiac death, sudden,
    automatic implantable
    cardioverter-defibrillator for,
    104
Cardiac output determination,
    noninvasive
    Doppler technology in, 72–75
    transthoracic electrical
        bioimpedance in, 75–79

Cardiac Output Monitoring and
    Diagnostic Unit (COMDU) for
    Jarvik-7, 134
Cardioverter-defibrillator,
    automatic implantable,
    101-116. See also Automatic
    implantable
    cardioverter-defibrillator
    (AICD)
Catheter, thermodilution, in
    cardiac output measurement,
    71–72
Closed-loop medication delivery
    system, 159–161
Clot formation
    in total artificial heart, 136
    in ventricular assist devices,
        131
Computer systems, clinical,
    15–16
    current approaches to, 16–17
    future directions in, 17–18
    problems with, 15–16
Consent, informed, 175–176
Continuous arteriovenous
    hemodialysis (CAVHD),
    153–154
Continuous arteriovenous
    hemofiltration (CAVH), 152
Continuous blood gas and
    electrolyte monitoring, 23–25
Continuous glucose monitoring,
    25–27
Continuous positive airway
    pressure (CPAP), 33
Continuous ST-segment
    analysis, 85–86
Continuous ultrafiltration
    therapy, 143–154. See also
    Ultrafiltration therapy,
    continuous
Control mode of ventilation,
    32, 34

Counterpulsation, balloon, 121–122
Convection in ultrafiltration, 146

## D

Death, cardiac, sudden, automatic implantable cardioverter-defibrillator for, 104
Diffusion in ultrafiltration, 146
Disease process, ethical decision making and, 184
Doppler cardiac output determination, 72–75

## E

Economic considerations of new technology, 165–166
Electrodes
  of automatic implantable cardioverter-defibrillator, 101, *102, 103*
  of external pacemakers, size and placement of, 93–94
Electrolyte monitoring, continuous, 23-25
Electronic Patient Information Chart (EPIC), 17
Electrophysiologic disturbances, automatic implantable cardioverter-defibrillator for, 105–106
EMTEK system 2000, 17
Environment, health care, current, 171–173
Ethical issues
  addressing
    action in, 190–192
    advocacy in, 190
    assessment in, 189–190

discussion on, 193
framework for, 188–193
nurse's role in, 187–188
autonomy vs. paternalism as, 177–180
disease process and, 184
factors affecting, 183–187
family wishes and, 185
hospital policies and, 187
identification of, 173–183
justice vs. utilitarianism as, 180–181
legal issues and, 187
patient feelings/wishes and, 185
patient needs and, 183–184
patient rights and, 184–185
professional integrity vs. personal integrity as, 183
resource allocation and, 186–187
society and, 186
treatment team and, 186
veracity vs. fidelity as, 181–182
External pacemakers, 91–96
  characteristics of, 91–94
  effectiveness of, 94
  electrode size and placement for, 93
  history of, 91
  implementing, 94–96
  myocardial injury from, 94
  pacing modes of, 94
  pacing threshold of, 92
  pulse duration and strength from, 92–93

## F

Family wishes, ethical decision making and, 185

Fiberoptic systems in blood gas monitoring, 25
Fidelity vs. veracity, 181–182
Filtrate column, ultrafiltration and, 149
Fluid replacement, ultrafiltration and, 148–149
Fluorescence, optical, in blood gas monitoring, 25

## G

Glucose monitoring, continuous, 25–27

## H

Health care environment; current, 171–173
Heart, artificial, 122, 132–137. See also Artificial heart, total (TAH)
Hematocrit, ultrafiltration and, 147–148
Hemodialysis, arteriovenous, continuous, 153–154
Hemodynamics of total artificial heart, 134–135
Hemofilter in continuous ultrafiltration therapy, 145
High-frequency ventilation (HFV), 32
Hospital policies, ethical decision making and, 187

## I

Infection
    potential for, in ventricular assist devices, 131
    total artificial heart and, 136
Informed consent, 175–176

Integrity, professional vs. personal, 183
Intermittent mandatory ventilation (IMV), 33, 34
Intragastric pH monitoring, 25–27
Inverse ratio ventilation (IRV), 38–42
    effects of, 40–41
    indications for, 41
    monitoring of, 42
Ion-sensitive field-effect transistors (ISFETs) in electrolyte monitoring, 23–24

## J

Jarvik-7 total artificial heart, surgical placement of, 134
Justice vs. utilitarianism, 180–181

## L

Lambert-Beer law, 54
Legal issues, ethical decision making and, 187
Life support, ethical issues of, 174–175
Light-emitting diodes (LEDs) of pulse oximeter transducer, 54, 55

## M

Mechanical ventilation, advances in, 31–47. See also Ventilation; Ventilators
Medication delivery systems, closed-loop, 159–161
Monitoring
    bedside, 23–27. See also Bedside monitoring

of inverse ratio ventilation, 42
of pressure support
ventilation, 38
ST-segment, 85–86
Myocardial injury from external
pacemakers, 94

## N

Noninvasive cardiac output
determination, 71–79. *See
also* Cardiac output
determination, noninvasive
Noninvasive Continuous
Cardiac Output Monitor
(NCCOM), 77–79
Nurse, role of, in addressing
ethical issues, 187–188

## O

Optical fluorescence in blood
gas monitoring, 25
Oximetry, pulse, 53–67. *See
also* Pulse Oximetry

## P

Pacemakers, external, 91–96.
*See also* External pacemakers
Pacing modes for external
pacemakers, 94
Pacing threshold for external
pacemakers, 92
Paternalism vs. autonomy,
174–175, 177–180
Patients
feelings/wishes of, ethical
decision making and, 185
needs of, ethical decision
making and, 183–184
rights of, ethical decision
making and, 184–185

pH monitoring, intragastric,
25–27
Photodiode of pulse oximeter
transducer, 54, 55
Plasma protein level,
ultrafiltration and, 147–148
Portable Nursing Unit Terminal
(PNUT), 17
Positive end-expiratory
pressure (PEEP), ventilators
and, 33, *34*
Pressure-cycled ventilators, 31
Pressure support ventilation
(PSV), *34*, 35–38
effects of, indications for,
37–38
monitoring of, 38
Professional integrity vs.
personal integrity, 183
Pulmonary artery balloon
pumping, 121-126
clinical studies on, 124
counterpulsation in, 121–122
experimental studies in,
123–124
future uses of, 124
nursing implications of,
125–126
for right ventricle, 123
Pulse duration and strength
with external pacemakers,
92–93
Pulse generator in automatic
implantable cardioverter-
defibrillator, 101
Pulse oximeters, dual-signal,
56
Pulse oximetry, 53–67
accuracy of, 61, 64
case studies on, 64–66
clinical application of, 56–57
clinical operation of, 57–58
display screen in, 58

patient care considerations
in, 61
potential problems with, 59,
61, *62–63*
principles of, 53–56
sensor in, 58–59, *60*
Puritan-Bennett 7200a
ventilator, 45–46

## Q

Quinlan, Karen, case of, 174

## R

Real cost determination for new
technology, 166
Renal failure, total artificial
heart and, 137
Resources
allocation of, ethical decision
making and, 186–187
scarce, allocation of, 174
Right ventricle, 123
failure of, pathophysiology
of, 123

## S

Siemens Servo 900C
ventilator, 46–47
Slow continuous ultrafiltration
(SCUF), 151–153
Societal changes, 173–176
Society, ethical decision
making and, 186
Sramek-Bernstein equation in
cardiac output measurement,
76–77
ST-segment analysis,
continuous, 85–86
Suction, ultrafiltration and,
149–150

Sudden cardiac death,
automatic implantable
cardioverter-defibrillator for,
104
Synchronized intermittent
mandatory ventilation (SIMV),
33, *34*

## T

Technological therapy, issues
related to, future of, 194
Technology
in critical care nursing,
historical development of,
310
chronology of, 4–7
future in, 9–10
past in, 3–9
today in, 9
new, economic considerations
of, 165–166
Thermodilution catheter in
cardiac output measurement,
71–72
Threshold, pacing, for external
pacemakers, 92
Thrombus formation
in total artificial heart, 136
in ventricular assist devices,
131
Time-cycled ventilators, 32
Tissue perfusion, decreased,
in ventricular assist devices,
131–132
Transducer of pulse oximeter,
54, *55*
Transthoracic electrical
bioimpedance (TEB) in
cardiac output determination,
75–79
Treatment team, ethical
decision making and, 186

## U

Ultrafiltrate collection circuit
anticoagulation of, 150
in continuous ultrafiltration
therapy, 145
Ultrafiltration therapy,
continuous, 143–154
blood flow and, 146–147
blood lines for, 144–145
filtrate column and, 149
fluid replacement and,
148–149
hematocrit and plasma
protein level and, 147–148
hemofilter for, 145
modalities of, 151–154
slow, 151–152
suction and, 149–150
technical design and setup
for, 143–145
ultrafiltrate collection circuit
for, 145
Utah Drive System II for
Jarvik-7 TAH, parameters on,
135–136
Utilitarianism vs. justice,
180–181

## V

Venous blood lines for
continuous arteriovenous
hemofiltration, 144–145
Ventilation
assist/control mode of,
32–33, *34*
control mode of, 32, *34*
intermittent mandatory, 33,
*34*
inverse ratio, 38–42
mechanical, advances in,
31–47

pressure support, *34*, 35–38.
*See also* Pressure support
ventilation (PSV)
synchronized intermittent
mandatory, 33, *34*
Ventilator(s)
Bear 5, 43–45
high-frequency, 32
modes for, 32–35
new generation, 42–47
pressure-cycled, 31
Puritan-Bennett 7200a,
45–46
Siemens Servo 900C, 46–47
time-cycled, 32
types of, 31–32
volume-cycled, 31–32
Ventricle, right, 123
failure of, pathophysiology
of, 123
Ventricular assist devices, *122*,
126–132
anatomical placement of,
127–128
clot formation in, 131
decreased tissue perfusion
in, 131–132
infection potential in, 131
modes of assistance in,
128–129
patient anticoagulation for,
129
pulsatile versus nonpulsatile
flow in, 128, *129*, *130*
right and left, 127
Ventricular tachycardia,
recurrent, automatic
implantable cardioverter-
defibrillator for, 105–106
Veracity vs. fidelity, 181–182
Volume-cycled ventilators,
31–32

# About the Editor

John Clochesy obtained a B.S.N. from Marian College of Fond du Lac and a M.S. in Medical-Surgical Nursing from the University of Wisconsin-Madison. He has 13 years of critical care nursing experience in a variety of clinical, educational, and administrative positions at St. Agnes Hospital, St. Joseph Hospital, the University of Wisconsin, the University of Arizona, Cedars-Sinai Medical Center, and the University of California, Los Angeles.

John is the author of numerous articles and book chapters. His first book, *Essentials of Critical Care Nursing,* was published by Aspen Publishers, Inc., in 1988. He serves on the editorial boards of *Critical Care Nursing Quarterly, Dimensions of Critical Care Nursing, Journal of Advanced Medical-Surgical Nursing,* and *Journal of Cardiovascular Nursing.* In addition, John serves as a reviewer for *Heart & Lung.*